Ray & Sue

Your friendship drawn
through the years has
been a true gift.

Archbishop Bordero

Spiritual
Living
in
Secular
Society

Spiritual Living in Secular Society

The Teachings of Archbishop William D. Borders

Cathedral Foundation Press
Baltimore, Maryland

Printed and bound in the United States of America.

1 2 3 4 5   05 04 03 02 01 00 99 98 97 96

Library of Congress Cataloging-in-Publication Data

Borders, William D., 1913-
    Spiritual living in secular society : the teachings of Archbishop William D. Borders.
          p.   cm.
    ISBN 1-885938-04-7 (cloth). - - ISBN 1-885938-06-3 (pbk.)
    1. Catholic Church - - Doctrines.   I. Title.
BX1751.2.B59   1996
230'.2 - - dc20   96-29332
                                         CIP

Published in 1996 by

Cathedral Foundation Press
P.O. Box 777
Baltimore, Maryland 21203

Publisher: Daniel L. Medinger
Press Director: Gregg A. Wilhelm
Assistant Manager: Patti Medinger
Book design: Sue Seiler
Cover design: Steve Fabijanski
Cover photograph: Denise Walker

CONTENTS

Spiritual Living in Secular Society

FOREWORD

Officially retired, Archbishop William Donald Borders is a wonderfully active Bishop who now presents his teaching of God's word in printed form.

In lectures to clergy, religious and laity, the Archbishop for years has offered guidance on how to grow spiritually in the face of contemporary culture's many pressures. His wise, practical and inspiring counsels, gathered into this book, should bring great benefit to many, many readers.

Of special note are the ways in which the author draws upon major themes of the Second Vatican Council and, at the same time, stresses very down-to-earth themes such as our need to practice the virtue of humility and to be aware and open to the power of God's grace.

May this book be an occasion for God's grace to touch the hearts of those who come in faith to read its pages.

William Cardinal Keeler
Archbishop of Baltimore
August, 1996

INTRODUCTION

The first time I met Archbishop William Borders, I was interviewing for the job as editor of the *Catholic Review*. Dutifully, I was waiting to meet with the search committee when a man in a cleric suit, but a gray pullover sweater, approached and said hello. I spoke to him casually and familiarly, neither of us identifying ourselves. Imagine my surprise when minutes later I was introduced to the Archbishop of Baltimore—and it was the same man that I had been speaking to so calmly earlier.

Archbishop Borders is an unassuming man. The fact that his episcopal chain was covered by a sweater on that February morning would have meant little to him. Interestingly, a few years later, after being hired as editor of his archdiocesan newspaper, I asked him if he remembered anything about that day when we first met. He was direct. "I was impressed," he said, "that I asked you a question that you couldn't answer and you were confident enough to tell me 'I don't know.' "

For me, this anecdote speaks volumes about my relationship with the thirteenth Archbishop of Baltimore and his relationship with many others. Because he is a quintessential humble man and he respects humility in others. (Frankly, I don't think my 'I don't know response' speaks so well of me; more likely I was simply too discombobulated to come up with a quick answer.) Then, slightly more than a decade after our first encounter I again met up with Archbishop Borders in the very same hallway and he said he was thinking about publishing a book of the lecture series he had been giving around the country since he retired in 1989. I asked if he had considered having it published by Cathedral Foundation Press, a relatively new book publishing division of the *Catholic Review*. His humility came through loud and clear as the archbishop asked me if the Press would be interested. I assured him. Then we discussed who would edit the book for him and we ran down the list of those who had assisted his writings as archbishop. After going over the usual suspects, he said, "I think I'd be most comfortable with you." This was the second time the archbishop had hired me. And I was very pleased.

The wonder of my job as an editor in the Catholic press is that it has given me not just a ringside seat to events and issues in our church, but it also has given me a first rate education in Roman Catholicism. My daily life is meeting with people who are shaping and implementing Catholic teaching. So I jumped at the chance to edit this book.

However, Archbishop Borders laid down only one ground rule for my job as editor. "I want you," he said, "to challenge me on anything you think doesn't make sense, is wrong or in error." Simple ground rules, but a daunting task. I am pleased to report that our time together was sometimes vigorous, but there was never any doubt who had the upper hand. We went over ideas, concepts, sentence structure, and word choice. And what you will read in this book is the teachings of Archbishop Borders. If you haven't met him, you will through this book. You will not get the opportunity for follow up questions like I did, but I am hopeful that you will find a framework for study of our faith, your faith, and the future of the faith. This book is designed to serve the needs of serious students and fellow seekers along the journey.

In this book, Archbishop Borders has latched on to the key issue of our times—the development of conscience. This book is linear exploration of the formation of a good conscience. For many people, development of a good conscience is a lost art, an endeavor not worthy of a life's work. In this book, readers will find a solid basis in scripture, church teachings, modern psychology and sociology, and common sense to stimulate growth and maturity. The teachings, clearly presented, come from an archbishop who has faced the challenges of his time in the context of eternal truths.

Archbishop Borders is a shepherd formed by his times. He grew up on a depression era Midwestern farm, provided pastoral ministry to a world at war, and nurtured college students on the brink of social and cultural revolution. A participant in the Second Vatican Council, he served as a founding bishop of a diocese and then was named archbishop of the oldest diocese in the United States. In this book, an amplification of a series of lectures, Archbishop Borders reveals his optimism about his unassailable hope in the Risen Lord. He also explores the challenges of secularism to the development of a community of faith. Finally, he presents a pragmatic approach to helping individuals reach a peace that only belief in Jesus can bring.

If you enjoy this book, I am pleased. I only ask you to share the joy that I have had in recent months working closely with this revered and respected leader of the Catholic Church to whom I not only owe so much, but whom I greatly admire.

Daniel L. Medinger
Publisher
Cathedral Foundation Press
August, 1996

Prologue

Father Walter Burghardt, who in my judgment is a homilist almost without peer of this generation, tells of advice he received, while a young priest, from Father John Courtney Murray, an influential theologian of Vatican II. He was having difficulty finding an introduction for a talk he was to give in the near future. Father Murray responded to his request for help with an insight that remained with Father Burghardt for forty years. "Walter, tell them what you are going to say, then say it, and then tell them what you have said."

In writing this book, I am in a similar position. In the beginning I had no intention of writing a book; I was just going to develop a series of classes attempting to help people cope with a secular society while trying to live a spiritual life. However, many who attended these classes suggested that I publish my lectures in book form. This effort will succeed only if the readers understand and appreciate their capacity to love and their ability to transcend the physical and material aspects of life, both in time and eternity.

For as long as we have recorded history, people of each century have judged that their problems and pressures were peculiar to the generation in which they lived. However, in relationship to human limitations, one generation is not too different from another; but with regard to the pressures and problems, each generation and century is very different. This is certainly true of our generation.

During our time on this planet earth we have experienced conditions that are unique in the history of humankind. The explosion of knowledge, instant communication, the development of atomic research that gives the possibility of the annihilation of our world as we know it are peculiar to our century, if not to our generation. Social upheavals have brought about changes and a breakdown of Christian civilization and culture to the extent that objective moral values are not accepted, either theoretically or practically, in the judgment of so many of this world's population. Political pressures and the entertainment industry have either condoned or promoted pre-marital sex and homosexuality. The business world and industry have experienced insider trading and corporate takeovers to the detriment of the poor and the common good.

In reflecting on these conditions, I asked myself: How can any Christian, or any other religious person, live a life of peace and happiness in the face of these pressures and accepted lack of values?

A few years ago I was giving a series of talks at a major seminary and one of the professors with a skeptical turn of mind asked the question: "How can you possibly suggest answers to these difficulties in a course of twelve lectures?" I hope that his kindly expressed skepticism did not reflect presumption on my part or the inevitable judgment that I was not living in the real world.

However, the professor does have a point, and it rests in both the diverse and different understandings of human freedom and the misuse of freedom. Freedom will always be the central quality of human culture and concern, because it is the guarantee of the dignity of the human person and the bond of unity in society. In Sacred Scripture, both St. John and St. Paul addressed this reality. St. Paul tells us that we are made free for freedom. St. John tells us that "the truth shall make you free."

Possibly my starting point should have been that this world belongs to God and that He called us into being so that we could live in freedom in this life, which is only a limited journey, and ultimately to respond to the call to know God as He is in the world to come. As men and women of faith, we accept the truth that God provides the means not only for us to cope with difficulties, but also, through grace and revelation, to find happiness and fulfillment through His providence, which is greater than the weakness and malice of any person or of any culture.

For that reason, I want to present an understanding of the Church as presented in the great documents of Vatican II, *Lumen Gentium* ("The Constitution of the Church") and *Gaudium et Spes* ("The Church in the Modern World"). These documents clearly portray God's presence in our lives, the power of grace in our decision-making, and an understanding of priorities and values. The recent publication of the Catechism of the Church in some eight hundred pages spells this out in such a manner that if I had any doubt as to how the Church explains Christ's teachings under the inspiration of the Holy Spirit, I have a resource that will challenge my thinking regardless of any culture or circumstance of life.

The Catechism quotes *Lumen Gentium* describing the Church in the following manner: "The Church essentially is both human and divine, visible but endowed with invisible realities, zealous in action and dedicated to contemplation, present in the world, but as a pilgrim, so constituted that in her the human is directed towards and subordinated to the divine, the visible to the invisible, action to contemplation, and this present world to the city yet to come, the object of our quest" (*Lumen Gentium* 8).

Just as God is a mystery, so also the Church is a mystery — a reality of God that we experience but cannot fully understand. We who are the Church exist in history, but at the same time transcend it.

However, I am a human being, created in the likeness of God, and in my spiritual soul God has given me a free will and has placed me in charge of my own destiny. This is both my dignity and my challenge. To clarify my thinking I must make the philosophical distinction between free will and freedom, and freedom and liberty. Sometimes people confuse the three. No one can enter into the soul of another and take away his or her free will. Personal freedom is a result of a person using that free will to choose that which is good. However, freedom is often limited by the constraints of other ideologies, policies and laws, but God has granted us an intellect that can cope with these restraints and limitations. Still, I am a sinful man, and I kind of suspect that you also have been guilty of sin. Therefore, my next step in coping with the secular society is accepting and understanding the redemptive love of God that we call grace. God is always present within us; the power of His love moving in our very being enables us to rise above our own limitations and the pressures of society.

In our journey through life, we are confident that our life has meaning and purpose, but we know that perfection is not of this world. Yet in the human psyche there is a longing for perfect happiness. St. Augustine, writing in the fourth century, expressed this so well: "Our hearts are longing for you, O Lord, and will not rest until they rest in you." This hope of every person is rooted in the seeking of a total security, a love that lasts in an unclouded happiness. This longing has never been completely fulfilled, but stays with us whatever we may do, and for a religious person sets the tone for every day of our lives.

Since this longing for fulfillment is inherent and constant in our very being, it is meant to be fulfilled. From revelation we know that this longing comes from the creative and redemptive love of God. St. Paul tells us in his Letter to the Romans: "God's love has been poured into our hearts, through the Holy Spirit" (Romans 5:5). This love is what we traditionally call sanctifying grace. It is the mystery of our personal relationship with God.

However, we are rational beings who make judgments and follow our consciences. Conscience is not some inner voice telling us to do something or not to do something; that something is good or something is bad. Conscience is an active judgment based on our knowledge of human nature and the truths revealed by God. Therefore, conscience must be informed, and as an adult I cannot rely purely on God's revelation as I learned as a child. I must read and study as an adult in order to live in the real world.

To live in the real world, I must go beyond philosophy, sociology, psychology and the empirical sciences. Not one of these disciplines, or all of them collectively, can answer the question of the meaning of life: Why was I born? Is there life after death? Therefore, I must ask the question: Has God revealed these answers to me? In the process of this analysis, I must recognize that God has revealed Himself and has offered the gift of faith.

To understand the nature of faith, we need to consider how certain can we be in any judgment? What is the relationship between science and philosophy? How do faith and reason work together? Most people are surprised that practically all knowledge comes through human faith: a knowledge of history and a knowledge of human relationships. Even for most of us our scientific knowledge depends on confidence and faith in the research of others, not on our own primary research. From an understanding of human faith, its strengths and limitations, we more easily move to an understanding of divine faith, which is the disposition by grace that enables us to recognize eternal truths. This is an ongoing process throughout our lives.

Thank God our eternal salvation does not depend on the level of knowledge that we have. The most primitive of peoples are loved by God equal to the more sophisticated, and therefore every person through the gift of faith can have sufficient knowledge to make a judgment in the circumstances in which he or she lives.

The greatest difficulty that we have in this journey through life is coping with problems and pressures often spurred by personal ambition, which is a terrible sin of pride. To address this reality, we need to understand how grace and revelation work together in personal growth through the virtue of humility. A humble person judges himself in relation to God, and in that process understands that separated from God life has little meaning and purpose. Humility is not just an ideal which remains static, but an attitude and insight that pervades every decision and action of human relations. The gifts and virtues of faith and charity, united with humility, enable a person to live in the real world that belongs to God.

In the twelve chapters of this book, I hope to explore in some depth the reality that God so created us that we can relate with each other in love, friendship, and support, and thus rise above the limitations and lack of values within the society in which we live. This is possible because Christ shares with us His own Divine Life.

You might suggest that in making this claim I am too simplistic and forgetting that our relationship with God is a mystery. You might also hold, as the poet expresses, that "I would go where angels fear to tread." The poet may be right but, my dear reader, may I make a counter suggestion that we proceed forward, but cautiously. If we go one step at a time, building the theory as one concept follows another, we will be on solid grounds, not resting on assumptions. We not only pursue these realities in thought, but also in prayer. Surely, the spiritual and supernatural life requires prayer.

A writer, or anyone who tries to share ideas and ideals, must find a common ground with others in order to move forward. May I suggest that our common ground, our starting point, will be the Church as we understand it from Vatican II. The Church cannot be defined, but can be described. The first chapter will approach that description.

Chapter I

The Nature of the Church

In the eleventh century, St. Anselm of Canterbury coined a definition of theology that probably has not been improved upon in the succeeding centuries. In his understanding of human nature and the gift of faith, he defined theology as *fides quaerens intellectum*—that is, faith in search of understanding. We are that Faith Community (i.e., the Church) and we are in search of understanding. Let us go back to the beginning.

Unconsciously, because of the dramatic change in the apostles at the first Pentecost when St. Peter spoke in Jerusalem to visitors from most of the countries of the then-civilized world, and these visitors listened and believed, we think of the first Pentecost as being the birthday of the Church. However, this is not accurate, for during the life of Christ He called the apostles and many other disciples, men and women, to form the new covenant which is the Church. At Pentecost the apostles received the grace, the courage, and the communication ability to proclaim the Gospel message beyond the close-knit community that had been theirs until Christ's resurrection and ascension.

In reading the Gospels, it is very clear that Our Lord surrounded Himself with many followers, both men and women, who in turn responded to the new covenant relationship. You will remember from your knowledge of Sacred Scripture the questions Jesus asked of the apostles: "Who do men say I am?"and "Who do you say that I am?" Their response indicated that they, in turn, began to understand who they were and how they were different as a group from their neighbors of the ancient Hebrew covenant. The response of the apostles to the question of Christ indicated their struggles with the mystery of the Incarnation, the union of the divine and human nature of Christ in the person of Jesus. They responded: "You are the son of man, the Son of God, the anointed one, the long-awaited Messiah."

The Gospels (especially St. Mark's) reflect their gradual self-awareness as a new community—i.e., a gradual understanding of themselves as a chosen band, a new people with a unique covenant relationship with God. This new covenant relationship and the new beginnings after the Ascension and Pentecost were highlighted in the year 70 by the destruction of the Temple and the resulting major crisis within the Jewish community. Fifteen years later, in the year 85, the Christian faith communities, who had accepted so many Gentile converts, were expelled from the synagogues. This traumatic rejection by the leaders of the Jews probably occasioned the new identification of the followers of Christ who were to be called Christians.

Today as a Christian people reflecting on our origins, we must continue to go back to our sources: Scripture; tradition; reason; and experiences as Church through almost two thousand years. Scholars have shared with us their understanding of the many Christian communities that developed under the inspiration of the Holy Spirit. Even though in ancient times these communities were isolated one from the other, nevertheless they had a unity through the bonding of the gift of faith and charity.

Now we, as did the early Christians in developing Liturgies for fifty-two weeks of the year, follow in the Liturgy of the Word the birth, life, teaching, passion, death, resurrection, and ascension of Our Lord Jesus Christ. In conjunction with and following the feasts of the Ascension and Pentecost, we again recall, through Sacred Scripture, the outreach of the Apostolic Church with the mission to proclaim eternal truths revealed by Christ and to provide opportunities to share in His redemptive love.

As we begin to consider the nature of the Church, we must first recognize that the Church is a mystery, a reality and truth that we cannot fully understand. It cannot be defined; it can only be described. Although we are limited and have a finite mind, we are not solely dependent on our own ability, for Christ is still dynamically present in the Church, we progress in our understanding and appreciation of the wonderful reality of salvation history. From the time of the Apostles to the present, images and symbols are used in Sacred Scripture and Tradition to assist us in understanding the reality of the Divine Life within the community that we call the Church.

Let us again go back almost two thousand years as our starting point and listen to St. Peter's description of the Church: "You are a chosen race, a royal priesthood, a holy nation, a people set apart, whom God claims for His own, to proclaim the glorious works of the One Who called you from darkness into light" (1 Peter 2:9).

St. Peter was not speaking from the point of view of theory; he clearly stated that we are a Church because we are called and are empowered by God. Our mission is to work toward the fulfillment of the mission for which Christ came into the world. St. Peter called for the first-century Christians, and also us, to share in each other's life and ideals, prayers and questions, rejoicing and mourning. This does not mean that we, the community of believers, the Church, are required to live together or act in a structured manner or to arrive at the same conclusions in mundane affairs. However, since God is the source of our faith and of our capacity to love, we are disposed by faith and are required by love to share our belief in eternal truths and to share spiritual values and ideals.

Remember Christ told us: "I am the vine and you are the branches." In accepting the gift of faith, a person is disposed to seek the common good rather than selfish interests. St. Luke, in the Acts of the Apostles, in substance wrote the first book of Church history, and in so doing clearly considered the faith community as one spiritual family. He perceives this community as an action of God opening the hearts of all mankind to the divine message of salvation.

Now, we should ask ourselves this question: To what extent have we as a Church attained this happy spiritual relationship?

I would like to enlarge on this question, first by a hypothetical question of a historian who does not have the gift of faith; and then by friendly questions of a theologian who has a love for the Church.

First, a historian of religion—evaluating with cold neutrality the structure and phenomena, the successes and the failures of the Church—might ask some penetrating questions: How does the Church of today claim to be the same as the primitive Church established by Christ? If the Church is divinely instituted and directed, should she not have been much more successful? Does the Church have the vitality to move in a secular society and emerge with supernatural convictions and provide a positive influential force?

Let us look to history. Nearly two thousand years after the death of Christ, we verify statistically the fact that there are more pagans, or at least non-Christians, than Christians in the world. Furthermore, among Christians tremendous divisions exist. This division, initiated in the sixteenth-century revolts led by Luther and Calvin, was followed by the eighteenth-century denial of the divinity of Christ, and, finally, by a modern denial of the existence of God Himself. Catholics and other Christians have been so affected by these positions that a high percentage of Christians can be considered merely nominal.

Let me now share with you the thought-provoking analysis of Father Henri de Lubac, a Vatican II theologian, and I quote: "I am told that she [the Church] is holy, yet I see her full of sinners. I am told that her mission is to tear man away from his earthly cares, to remind him of his eternal vocation, yet I see her constantly preoccupied with the things of the earth and of time, as if she wished to live here forever. I am told that she is universal, as open as divine intelligence and charity, and yet I notice that very often her members, through some sort of necessity, huddle together timidly in small groups...as human beings do everywhere. She is hailed as immutable, alone stable and above the whirlpools of history, and then, suddenly, under our very eyes, she upsets many of the faithful by the suddenness of her renewals."

Obviously Father de Lubac recognizes and accepts the ideals of St. Peter, but he is convinced that we as a Church have not yet fully attained these ideals. I think that we can learn from both St. Peter and Father de Lubac. While the Church is divine, it is also human, and therefore limited. The goal and true character of the Church is not found by turning in on itself and being primarily concerned in promoting its own welfare, but rather its concern in every century is for Christ's purpose—i.e., the redemption of people and cultures from sin and self-seeking. Therefore, it is not primarily numbers that are important, but rather the quality of influence in every aspect of human life. The Church is called to be a leaven for society in every century, in every generation. This can be accomplished only by faith in Jesus Christ and the truths He revealed, coupled with living a life of love that He shares with us.

St. Paul in a Letter to the Romans speaks of these needs in question form: "How can they believe unless they have heard of Him? How can they hear unless there is someone to preach?" The "someone," that is "us," must also be united with Christ as was St. Paul when he said: "I live, now not I, but Christ lives in me" (Galatians 2:20). It is the Word of God that changes the life of people, and the love of God that empowers.

People and cultures change, and in these changes throughout two thousand years the Holy Spirit is present as a constant guide.

Christ revealed truth in principle, in a Semitic language, in a rural culture. The truths that He revealed are eternal and do not change, but the language He used and the culture in which He lived are not constant. Languages and cultures change in every generation.

A couple of examples hopefully will illustrate how cultures and conditions of time and place help or limit the understanding and sharing of revealed truths in the circumstances of life. The United States of America is a relatively young country, only slightly over two hundred years old. Yet, life styles and availability of information have radically changed during these two hundred years. Even up to my own grandparents' time, most people lived in a rural environment. Communication beyond twenty miles was very limited. Even newspapers were not available in most areas. Libraries were few and far between. The sharing of all knowledge, including religion, reflected the knowledge and influence of few people.

A similar condition exists in many parts of the world in our own generation. About forty years ago I spent the summer replacing a Maryknoll priest in a small village in Guatemala. The residents were a very friendly Indian tribe who were open to me, a stranger among them. As visiting priest, I discovered that university teaching experience did not prepare me for any effective evangelization. Ninety-eight percent of the people could neither read nor write. Most of them had never left their mountain villages. There were the poorest people I have ever known. Any example from history that I could use, taken from the broader world or personal experience, was not helpful to them. Fortunately, a very kindly, intelligent but uneducated man moved in to help. The summer was not a total loss. We parted friends, and I learned that the gift of faith and love that comes to all people regardless of the circumstances of life cannot be measured by human limitations or education.

How can we continue to learn more about Jesus Christ and the truths that He revealed almost two thousand years after He lived on this earth? God and Jesus have always been understood through the prism of human minds, limited in what they can grasp, and by the interpretive skills of their times. God reveals Himself in creation, in history, particularly in the history of Israel, and in the life of Jesus and of His teaching, and down through the centuries in His Church. Every statement of doctrine (i.e., the Church teaching the Gospel message) must, of necessity, be within the context and understanding of the language and culture of each period of history, while reflecting on the truths Christ revealed.

In apostolic times, seeking to understand God was in the framework of Semitic categories of the mid-East. This certainly was different than the approach to understanding God two or three hundred years later in a culture dominated by the thought of Plato (e.g., St. Augustine's methodology). Still later, the magnificent synthesis of St. Thomas Aquinas, who used the categories of Aristotle, is different than the synthesis of today which must be correlated with the physical and social sciences. Two all-embracing documents of Vatican II are useful for us today to understand the Church and her mission. Those documents are *Lumen Gentium* ("The Constitution on the Church") and *Gaudium et Spes* ("The Church in the Modern World").

A question still remains: How do we who are limited remain faithful to His teaching? The Holy Spirit continues to work in the Church. With this guidance, the doctrinal explanation of each generation is a true presentation of revealed truth, but does not exhaust truth. These explanations of doctrine represent the limited insight of one period of Church history which can be modified and developed in another period of Church history. Truth never changes, but the explanation of revealed truth is approached from different directions in different periods and from different cultures, and in different languages.

The source of supernatural truths is God, and the power to accept and live according to these truths is the redemptive love of Christ. Each person, however, accepts these truths and this love in the natural process of learning and acquires an insight into their nature and depth, one judgment at a time. This human element is evident in the varied responses of grace and love. Had the members of the society of the Church entirely fulfilled the order of love left by Christ, one might think that the entire world would now be Christian. But the fact is that down through the years they and we have been deficient, and today we do not live up to the human potential that Christ offers in His redemptive love. For by strange paradox, the Church in each generation has asked her members to renounce the world for eternal life, and at the same time to become so united to the world as to make of it a society in which justice and charity would be dominant in all persons. A recognition of the dignity of the human person is implicit in such a society.

Therefore, the Church is not a static institution, but a living vital Mystical Body of Christ—the People of God on a pilgrimage through time to eternity. Christ tells us: "I am the Way, the Truth, and the Life." This is not a poetic expression, but a supernatural reality. Christ literally shares His divine life with us. Therefore, Christianity and the Church while internal in its members is external in its structure. The bond of faith and love, not structures, holds us together as a faith community. Structures are the expression of this bonding, not the cause.

In every century, the faith of individual members of the Church have had a positive relationship to every Christian of every age. The relationship is transcendent, but is expressed in the culture of each period, through the symbolism, the language, the music and art, as well as the thought content that is the heritage of each nation. Eternal truths revealed by God are received in a definite language with the limitation of that language, with the restraining influence of tribal or national customs, and with the particular prejudices of the history immediately preceding.

The Church is a mystery, a mystery of God's presence with us experienced with a vitality of warmth and love. However, there are some different ways to picture the Church's structure, as developed by Father Avery Dulles, S.J., a well-known theologian who specializes in ecclesiology, as outlined in his book, *Models of the Church.* The five models Father Dulles describes are:
1. The Church as an Institution;
2. The Church as Mystical Communion;
3. The Church as Sacrament;
4. The Church as Herald;
5. The Church as Servant.

It is clear that these models are not exclusive. Each model interrelates with the other models, but one remains dominant. This approach to this understanding of the Church is a dialectic rather than doctrinal theology. It is an approach that reflects the richness and diversity of the Church. While I am using Father Dulles' models, the descriptive approach is pretty much my own. He develops the models much more comprehensively.

The Church as Institution

Since the Church is a society, the Church needs the structure of government to exist and relate to other societies. In institutional ecclesiology, the function of the Church is usually divided into three powers and functions: teaching; sanctifying; governing. Christ appointed the Apostles as the first bishops and promised to remain with the Church until the end of time. The Church would be visible and its members would be baptized people who accept the universal teaching of truths, participate in the sacramental life, and are bonded by the love that Christ shares. Since the Church is a mystery, we recognize that as an institution we do not know all the answers, and therefore must recognize and accept our limitations.

The Church as Mystical Communion

Several theologians maintain that the Church has an inner core as community, or People of God, and an outer core as society. These theologians would hold that the inner core is the "real Church" and coincides with the scriptural images of the "Kingdom of God" and the "Communion of Saints." This would be a fellowship of people with God and with one another in Christ.

In the nineteenth century this fellowship was expressed by the scriptural image "The Mystical Body of Christ," as found in St. Paul's letters to the Romans (see chapter 12) and in 1 Corinthians (chapter 12 of that book, as well). In this analogy with the human body, the Church has an intrinsic vital principle which can grow, repair itself, and adapt itself to changing needs. St. Augustine, writing at the turn of the fourth century, developed the image of the Body of Christ with a stress on the mystical and invisible communion that binds together all those who are enlivened by the grace of Christ. This would include angels, members who are in heaven, and those outside the Church who are enlivened by the grace of Christ. This model has the value of inter-personal relationships and communal life, but at the same time, if overemphasized, could lead to a subjective approach which could change with the atmosphere of a given culture.

The Church as Sacrament

The concept of the Church as Sacrament certainly is not new, and can be recognized in the writings of St. Cyprian, St. Augustine, and St. Thomas Aquinas. However, this ecclesiology emerged in full clarity in our own century. Father Henri de Lubac, a *peritus* of the Second Vatican Council, has made a major contribution to this theory. He, as most students of the Church, would hold that the divine and human in the Church can never be disassociated. Writing in 1950, he stated: "If Christ is the Sacrament of God, the Church is for us the Sacrament of Christ; she represents Him, in the full and ancient meaning of the term, she really makes Him present. She not only carries on His work, but she is His very continuation, in a sense far more real than that in which it can be said any human institution is its founder's continuation."

The Church as a basic sacrament of Christ is stated in a number of documents of Vatican II. We are all familiar with the definition of a sacrament from the Council of Trent: "A sacrament is the visible form of an invisible grace." Various Councils have said, in essence, that the sacraments contain the grace they signify and confer the grace they contain.

The Church becomes an actual event of grace when it appears most concretely as a sacrament—that is, in actions of the Church whereby men and women are bound together by grace in a visible expression.

The Church as sacrament is a living community of the grace of Christ. This grace will impel people to prayer, confession, worship, and other acts whereby the Church externally realizes its essence. Through these actions, the Church signifies what it contains and contains what it signifies. The Church thus becomes an event of grace as the lives of its members are transformed in hope, in joy, in self-forgetful love, in peace, in patience, and in all other Christian virtues. However, because of human limitation, the Church never fully achieves itself, and through the guidance of the Holy Spirit is always in process.

The Church as Herald

The ecclesiology that considers the Church as Herald concentrates on the "Word of God" rather than "Sacramental Presence." The mission of the Church is to proclaim that which it has heard, believed and has been commissioned to proclaim.

This model is radically centered on Jesus Christ and on the Bible as the primary witness to Him. The Church's mission is to proclaim the Word of God to the whole world. All the Church needs to do is to teach the Word with integrity and persistence. Everything else is secondary. The community, or Church, happens wherever the Spirit breathes. This understanding could lead to a radical depreciation of the institutional and historical elements of the Church. It also could focus too exclusively on witness to the neglect of action.

The Church as Servant

"The Pastoral Constitution of the Church in the Modern World" outlines a new understanding of the Church in our modern day. It recognizes the contributions of the various cultures and the influences of both the physical and social sciences. It asserts that the Church should consider itself as part of the total human family sharing the same concerns as the rest of humankind.

Christ came into the world not to be served but to serve; so the Church, carrying the mission of Christ, seeks to serve the world by fostering a community that includes all people. Cardinal Richard Cushing of Boston, shortly after the conclusion of Vatican II, expressed the servant role very clearly: "Jesus came not only to proclaim the kingdom, He came also to give Himself for its realization. He came to serve, to heal, to reconcile, to bind up wounds. Jesus, we may say, is the exceptional Good Samaritan. He is the One Who comes alongside of us in our needs and in our sorrow; He extends Himself for our sake. He truly dies that we might live, and He ministers to us that we might be healed."

The Church not only announces the coming of the Kingdom in word through preaching and teaching, but definitively in work, in reconciliation, in service to the poor and alienated, and in healing the wounds of human misery. However, the Church must not look to itself as only a humanitarian social agency, or an organization that is available to respond to crisis situations. The Church must be the universal sacrament of salvation, the Body of Christ which has a mandate to serve. The Church must be a leaven for society and open to serve all people wherever they are.

Very briefly then, we have considered the Church from five different models or descriptions. There is always a danger in considering the positive and good of any model that we forget that each is incomplete in responding to the love and message of Christ in salvation history. We might even forget that the Church is a mystery and by over-emphasis fall into a modern type of gnosticism.

To summarize, within the institutional model, the official Church teaches, sanctifies, and guides with the delegated authority of Christ; in the communion model, the Church is viewed as God's people, or Christ's Body, growing into the final perfection of the Kingdom; in the sacramental ecclesiologies, the Church is understood as the visible manifestation of the grace of Christ in human community; in the herald model, the Church takes on an authoritarian role, proclaiming the Gospel as a divine message to which the world must listen; and in the servant model, the Church must discern the signs of the times, seek to operate as a liaison between the secular world and Christian tradition and become a catalyst for the change of structures for the common good. In our probing of the mystery of the Church, we need the insights of all these models—and possibly others not yet conceived—to offer to the finite world the infinite mystery of God's love in salvation history.

Each person attains happiness by growing in grace. In every pattern of history the love and grace of God is present; it is not limited by the attainments or abilities of men and women. The gift of faith and of love is personal to each individual. In any particular period of history, culture, or society, the grace of Almighty God disposes a person's intellect to arrive at a knowledge of revealed truths and to recognize them as revealed. It is not a perfect knowledge because a person's knowledge is limited, but when one does make a judgment, in faith, God's providential love offers security and protection. Recognizing truths as revealed, a person knows how to act, what virtues to practice in one's culture so that he or she can acquire happiness and peace, which is a guarantee of one's attainment of eternal happiness. This is the gift of faith and the gift of a share of the Divine Life that comes to us through the Church.

History has witnessed that Christ's promise is constant throughout the centuries, and the light of faith remains through the changing mists of these centuries and is alive today. Perhaps two hundred years from now scholars will look back at us as socially disoriented people and doubt our love of God. Then they will avert to Christ's institution of the

Church, knowing that because it is His society, it will endure to the end of time. The inadequacies of men and women do not limit the providence of God.

When Pope John XXIII called the bishops of the world to assemble in the Second Vatican Council, he said, "Distrustful souls see only darkness burdening the face of the earth. We instead like to reaffirm all our confidence in Our Savior, Who has not left the world He redeemed."

Up to this point, because of the transcendent nature of God and His relationship with us, I have been somewhat abstract. May I conclude this chapter with some practical suggestions from religious educators:

1. Christ taught a way of life, not a doctrine. Doctrine is a statement of the way of life as guided by the Holy Spirit.

2. Religious education is learning, not teaching.

3. Learning involves attitudes and behaviors as much as intellectual content.

4. Learning takes place primarily in life experience, not in schools or classrooms.

5. The family, the parish, and the community are the primary classrooms for religious education.

6. Adults are the most important students.

7. Parish programs must involve flexible efforts in helping people toward growth in family, parish, and community —living according to the Way of Life of Jesus Christ.

Our understanding of ourselves as a People of God and the day-by-day realization of our living as a Church will be put in a theoretical abeyance until the third chapter. The next chapter will treat the stark reality of secularism, which I hope will not be too depressing, but will indicate a need for us to become a spiritual society that is not apart from the secular world, but independent of the forces of that environment. We are called to be a spiritual leaven for the society in which we live. Remember, Jesus prayed to the Father: "I am not asking

You to take them out of the world, but I ask You to protect them from the evil one" (John 17:15).

Chapter II

The Harm of Secularism in Society

A thoughtful person of any period of history must seek to understand the society in which he or she lives. To-day this is even more imperative, because of the succeeding conflicts and disorders of past and current generations. New philosophies, new concepts of government, have emerged. Social upheavals have brought about a change and breakdown of civilization, and it seems that people have lost their unifying bond.

Within the short span of our adult lives, we have witnessed fratricidal conflicts and injustices that ancient pagan countries could hardly equal. With sadness I will recall to your minds obvious examples of these breakdowns of civilization, such as the continual murders in Northern Ireland; the fanatical leadership in Iran and the resulting loss of freedom and lives; the senseless and inconclusive war between Iran and Iraq, and subsequent invasion of Kuwait by Iraq and the tragic war in which we were involved; the continued devastation of Lebanon because of the intransigent factions of both Christians and Muslims; the continued hatred of Jews and Arabs for each other and the resulting conflicts; the breakup of Communist control of Eastern European countries and some positive yet, confusing results, that have followed; and the breakup of Yugoslavia and the establishment of separate republics. Civil war has erupted in a manner that will parallel atrocities of almost any period of history.

Within our own country we have experienced moral deterioration on many levels, and we do not yet know the ultimate results. Consider the continuing ramifications of the Watergate scandal and other instances of the misuse of political power and influence; consumerism and the exaggerated desire for creature comforts; last year, one percent of the income of the wealthy equaled forty percent of income earned by those on the lower level; insider trading and ruthless takeovers of companies inevitably lead to the loss of jobs held by long-time employees; the widespread drug sub-culture and the accompanying devastation of families, violence, and death; the public acceptance of promiscuity and homosexuality; the fact that half of all marriages end in divorce, and twenty-seven percent of second marriages; and the thousands of babies killed each year by abortion. These conditions have not happened suddenly, but are the result of a gradual erosion of Christian values and the lessening of belief and practice of religion.

Catholics bonded in faith and love are called to work with people of every walk of life, to proclaim the Gospel, offer an insight into the dignity of the human person, and to teach others that they were called into existence by God, and that the world belongs to God and we are temporary residents on this planet earth. We have accepted this reality, but the culture and atmosphere in which we live often makes our efforts counter-cultural.

Recently, a book was published titled *The Day America Told the Truth*. It was the result of a comprehensive survey and study with a margin of error of two to four percentage points. Among the findings: only thirteen percent of the populace still believes in all the ten biblical Commandments; nine out of ten citizens lie regularly; nearly one-third of all married Americans have had an affair; one-fifth of the nation's children have lost their virginity in their adolescent years; one-sixth of the adults say that they were physically abused as children (one in seven sexually abused); one woman in five says that she has been date-raped. Again, these conditions did not happened suddenly, but are the result of a gradual erosion of Christian values and the lessening of belief and practice of religion. Many factors have contributed to the loss of objective moral values and the loss of faith.

The structure of western society is of such a nature that the accidentals and conventions of Christianity have not disappeared, although the principles that gave rise to these structures have been lost. Lip service is often given without the acceptance of moral values. Without the principles upon which moral judgments are based, a philosophical grasp of reality has been lost. We live in an atmosphere of secularism and in a society wherein serious decisions are made on a pragmatic basis.

Secularism is such a pervading influence in today's culture that it is almost a narcissistic form of community self-worship affecting individual and policy decisions in every aspect of life. It would be difficult to define secularism because of the many contributing causes, but it can be described. Secularism is a condition of society whose structures try to exist without any religious basis. Civil power would claim to have autonomy independent of religious influence, and while for the most part not denying the existence of God, decisions are made without any reference to the truths He revealed.

A survey of the development and a history of the influence of secularism in the Western world would be a monumental task. Such a work of necessity would include studies of the Renaissance, the philosophies of Kant, Hegel and Marx, the naturalism of Rousseau and Darwin, and the psychologies of Watson and Freud. The scope and exacting character of such a work would require the time and effort of a great scholar working all his life, and for that reason all writers in the field limited themselves to particular areas.

Pragmatism, the most common expression of secularism,

in most instances is an effect more than a cause, inasmuch as most people who make pragmatic judgments do not avert to the philosophical assumptions underlying their judgments. The source and underlying cause rest in the theory of the self-existing secular world. Morality to the theoretical secularists is a human convention that necessarily changes with conditions, cultures, and circumstances. Their code or norm of behavior is that of expediency limited by decency.

Because of these assumptions that do not attribute human existence and nature to God, the theoretical secularist does not and cannot recognize the existence of a spiritual soul. This theory does not allow for the source of human dignity and freedom. Thus a person would be entirely the product of heredity and environment. A secularist transfers to secular authority education, economic justice, and other social functions recorded by historians as traditionally within the religious and family areas of responsibility.

The practical secularist, on the other hand, does not necessarily exclude the spiritual nature of a person, but concerns himself only with human existence in the order of time. He does not give priority of time and thought to man's relationship with God here and hereafter. He does not deny the spiritual nature of a person; he just does not consider it. This version of secularism is in effect a practical exclusion of God from human thinking and living.

Today, growing numbers of Christians lack a sense of sin because they do not have a realization of personal responsibility to God, which should be a moving force in their lives. Unless a man or woman has a personal relationship with God and a realization that God has called each person into existence and sustains one's being, he or she knows God only on the level of the abstract. Sin becomes then a breaking of rule, not a defiance of the creative love of God.

The effects of secularism, whether theoretical or practical, have reached into every unit of society—not only the family and political structure, but even religious commitment. The content of secularist thought has brought immeasurable disorder to the family. It has prevented an understanding of the sacred character of marriage with so many couples by removing from the marriage consent the covenant relationship with God. The will and convenience of the husband and wife have so often become the goal of marriage, rather than the stability of a lifelong relationship. The love of husband and wife is one of the great gifts of human relationship, but that love is never isolated from society as a whole inasmuch as everyone is called into being by God and bonded together by the love that Christ shares with us. In the public forum, a cynical disregard for the noble purpose of sexual intercourse has popularized practices which violate nature and rob human procreation of its dignity and nobility. A pseudo-science and selfish pursuit of pleasure have been substituted so often for salutary self-discipline in so much of family life. This type of secularism has in our society undermined the stability of the family as a divine institution and has given our country the greatest divorce problem in the Western world. Fifty-one percent of first marriages in the United States end in divorce, and twenty-seven percent of second marriages end in divorce. In taking a relationship with God out of family life, society's basic educational institution of marriage has been deprived of its most powerful means of teaching and sharing transcendental values to a child as he or she matures toward adult responsibility.

Every level of education has experienced the pressure and activity of secularism. In the United States, secularists have been quick to exploit for their own purposes the public policy adopted a century ago of banning the formal teaching of religion from the curriculum of our public schools. They have adopted this policy, which was initiated only as a practical solution to the problem of divided religious allegiance, and used it as a starting point in their philosophy of education. They attempt to exclude God from the schools and to apply the principle of Separation of Church and State as a legal sanction for their program of secularism.

In the rearing of children and in the formation of youth, omission is as effective as a positive statement. A philosophy of education which omits God necessarily draws a plan of life in which God has either no place or is a strictly private concern. There is a great difference between a practical arrangement which leaves the formal teaching of religion to the family and to the Church, which was the idea of Horace Mann (who might be called the father of public schools), and the educational theory of the secularist, who advisedly and avowedly excludes religion from the program of education. Both in theory and practice, the rights of parents and the Church in the field of education are denied or limited; the state is invested with almost supreme power. Educational monopoly is the ultimate objective of the secularist.

The impact of secularism on a social level is not limited to education. When the mass media are under the control of the secularist, the result is multiplied. The public press, interested in wide circulation, at times, gives descriptive details and pictures prurient in character, while at the same time on its editorial pages it emphasizes the grave problems of juvenile delinquency and drug problems. It strives for the sensational and presents to the reading public the weaknesses of human nature; often emphasizes the bizarre rather than the norm. Editorial policies concerning economic and social matters often reflect the thinking of economic power rather than justice. It is a sad reality that some elements of secularism have become imbedded in laws and structures. If we are to combat secularism, we not only need to help individuals grow spiritually, but also work towards changing systems and structures in the society in which we live and work.

We must have a realistic understanding of freedom, liberty, and responsible decision-making in the formation of a personal conscience. We men and women who have accepted and live our vocation as children of God have the intellect and spiritual resources to cope with systems and structures. We remember the promise and mandate of Christ given to the Apostles before He ascended into heaven: "Full authority has been given to Me both in heaven and on earth; go therefore and make disciples of all the nations. Baptize them in the name of the Father, and of the Son, and of the Holy Spirit. Teach them to carry out everything I have commanded you, and know that I am with you always, until the end of the world" (Matthew 28: 18-20).

Yet, with regret, you know from personal experience and lifelong associations that even with the presence of Christ within us freedom has been, is, and will be misused. Sin enters the world in our life situation. It is one thing to talk about secularism and philosophies in the abstract as instrumental causes, and another thing to experience the resulting hurt, harm and suffering in personal and social life. Evil exists, and sin is the cause.

The problem of evil has never been fully understood and, of course, never completely explained. Why do we rational creatures act so perversely and so destructively? Why do we commit sin? Some philosopher wrote that "sin is absurd in the sense that disease is absurd." However, we recognize disease as a result of our mortality. Sin is something very different, because it is a decision of the will, flows from the disordering of a person's spiritual powers. These decisions create disorder not only within the individual person, but also in structures of society. For example, each of us has been repelled by the abuse of an innocent child and frightened by the financial support of death squads supported by affluent groups to protect what they would consider a threat to their financial empires.

How does a Christian address these questions and problems? We know from revelation from the teaching of the Gospel and from personal experience that sin does not exist in things, but only in persons through a misuse of free will. Sin ultimately is not primarily an imperfection of a human being, but the turning away from God. Then real evil is not the transgression of a cold, lofty law, but an offense against personal love. Finally, it is not just an offense against another person, but an offense against our God, our Creator and Redeemer. Serious sin becomes a habit, not just a transgression; it is a type of slavery that leads to spiritual impotence. It leads one into a future refusal to love—to love God and to love our neighbor.

Since everything that comes from the creative love of God is good, sin only comes from the misuse or corruption of something that is good. St. Augustine, writing in the fourth century, gave us a profound analysis of sin: "Impelled by love of his own independence, a man turns away from the universal whole to the individual part. If he had followed God's guidance in the general course of nature, he would have been led along the best way by God's law. But now in his apostate pride, which is the beginning of sin, he tries to grasp something that is greater than the whole. Striving to master it by his own laws, he is thrust back into caring for a part. There is nothing greater than the whole. Hence when he desires something greater, he grows smaller" (*De Trinitate* XII, 14).

This substitution of something for God is the source of all sin. It is a form of idolatry. The reality of sin is above all an inward attitude. The deed, taken in isolation, does not tell everything, for there exists a breach of loyalty to God. Yet in our Faith Community we live in an atmosphere of the redemptive love, the mercy of God. There is always a call for repentance and conversion. "God wills all men to be saved and come to a knowledge of truth."

Since Christ has taught us that we were called into existence by God and created to His image and likeness with a destiny that is heaven, it seems ridiculous that we could be guilty of idolatry. I have heard people say, "I recognize my weaknesses and my violation of the commandments, but I have never been guilty of idolatry." Not so. Ultimately, when we choose ourselves rather than God, we are violating the First Commandment. For that reason, in the next chapter we must understand our great gift of free will and its capacity to love, and hopefully our understanding of free will, freedom, and liberty will lead to a grasp of who we are in relationship to God.

Chapter III

Free Will, Freedom, and Liberty

Every thinking person who seeks to mature to his or her potential in the order of nature tries to understand conditions which affect behavior and to uncover the causes of good and evil in society and personal life. In this quest, he or she may be exposed to conclusions of biology, psychology, sociology, or some of the other empirical sciences. Answers from these disciplines may be valid, but collectively they will be incomplete. An understanding of the purpose of life and the ability to direct one's life to that end goes far beyond the data and conclusions of these sciences. In the final analysis, each of us must ask and answer the question: "What kind of person do I choose to become?"

We who have accepted the gift of faith and continue to experience a union with God in grace know that a Christian life is characterized by a life of freedom. St. Paul tells us that we are made free for freedom. St. John in his Gospel makes it much stronger as he quotes Jesus: "The truth shall make you free" (John 8:32). Freedom, therefore, is not an end in itself. It is the capacity to fulfill one's deepest aspirations in choosing the true and the good.

The real task of human life is to attain that ultimate freedom. We were born without being asked; our human nature is a gift that is both limited in life and open to the purpose of existence—to know and love God and be in perfect union with Him in eternity. Each of us has but one life to live. Life's last question will always be: "When I have reached the moment of death, have I become the person God called me to be?"

The answer, of course, lies in the mystery of God and His

communication with us. Before we move into this area of revelation and grace, we must look to our own capacity to direct
our lives to that end. Let us consider the nature and relationship of free will, freedom, and liberty. Ultimately, each day
the basic questions of life have to do with the purpose of our
existence.

First: Why was I conceived and born?

Second: Am I able to understand who and what I am, and
also the nature of any human being (i.e., the people in this
world outside of myself)?

Third: Do I accept my personal responsibility to make the
basic decisions that will affect my journey through life; and,
therefore, do I have a free will?

The answer to the first question many of us realize is basic to our lives. You will remember from your early days of
studying religion that the Baltimore Catechism stated that
each and every one of us was created "to know, love, and
serve God in this world, and to be happy with Him in the
next." I do not think that we have improved much on this definition, but since we are limited and think in categories, we
need to have a deeper understanding of our capacity to
know, our ability to make free choices, and our experience of
love and grace.

These questions suggest that we consider in some depth
the ability to think and understand, which is the science of
epistemology—or, in other words, the truth value of human
knowledge. However, I know from university experience
that it took me an entire semester of two sessions a week to
adequately address this subject. In a subsequent chapter
which considers the relationship of divine and human faith
at least a schematic analysis of the thought process will be in-
cluded.

The third question involving personal responsibility is
central to life, character, integrity, and ultimately love relationship.

Every person is conscious that he or she is unique, different, and separate from everyone else who has been born into this world. Everyone has an inherent desire for happiness and fulfillment. Throughout life, either consciously or unconsciously there is a search for the meaning of life. In that search, there exists a spontaneous realization that each one can choose, make decisions, and to that extent is responsible for personal development. In this consciousness, while no one is responsible for human nature and the complexity and refinement of physical and spiritual components and relationships, every rational person is responsible for working toward fulfillment for who he or she is called to be.

For what and whom am I called to be? This most fundamental of all questions cannot be answered by the empirical sciences or philosophy, or of psychology, but only by the gift of faith—God communicating with us.

This leads us to the great spiritual gift of human nature—i.e., our free will and our capacity to love. Consider with me free will, freedom, and liberty; they should not be confused one with the other. The ability to make decisions and to direct our life is a spiritual quality of human nature that enables us to become the kind of person who can live in harmony with the order of God's creation, with our neighbor and the law of love which is the law of God. We continue to make many decisions each day, as well as those vocational decisions that will have so much influence on our happiness and determine the kind of person we would like to become.

The choices that we make involve both the manner in which we choose, and response to invitations and rejections from others, that have so much to do with our goals, values and dreams. For example, when I made the decision to be a priest, I also made the decision not to marry, not to become involved in a business career. I am not only choosing for myself who I want to be, but also myself within the mystery of my life—in my relationship with God and my relationship with others. Each person has made similar decisions that have directly affected his or her life and the lives of others.

Normally, in scholastic philosophy and psychology, free will would be technically defined as "a rational appetency or the power to strive for an intellectually perceived good and to shun an intellectually perceived evil." We recognize that the will always follows the intellect, for the intellect presents to us not only those elements of reality that we can understand, but also whether they are desirable and good. You will recognize these examples of will and intellect in action: resisting; selecting; deciding; resolving; detesting; preferring; consenting; approving; disapproving; feeling tempted; refraining; forcing oneself; hating; yielding; regretting; losing control; feeling inclined; refusing; loving; acceding; and ultimately choosing. All of these mental and volitional states and experiences involve attitudes or acts of will with regard to objects, persons and situations that we would judge to be good for ourselves, for others, and in harmony with the love of God. Therefore, free will is something different than freedom. Freedom results from decisions or acts of the will that are in harmony with our nature and with the will of God. Freedom is limited not only by our nature, but also by the constraints, pressures, injustices and rights and influences of the people in the society in which we live.

Freedom is central to every aspect of human life. Personal freedom, economic freedom, political freedom, national freedom, freedom of religion, freedom of the press, freedom of the arts, freedom of education—these concepts, qualities, desires and manifestations of man's spiritual nature have been the rallying cry for the oppressed as well as the slogan for the political demagogue. Freedom from hierarchy, freedom from authority, freedom from the bourgeois society, freedom from dictatorship—these objectives have proven to be the motivating drive of the rebel in society, the emotionally immature, as well as the leader against injustice.

Freedom will always be the central fact of human culture and concern because its possession is the expression and guarantee of the dignity of the human person and the bond of unity in society. The misuse of freedom by the individual or social group will bring unhappiness, disorder and chaos in the same proportion as the freedom is misused. Liberty goes beyond individual freedom and pertains to society as a whole. Liberty is the result of freedom properly exercised by the body politic; servitude is the result of freedom inordinately exercised or negated.

Liberty is a sign and acceptance of human worth, and a manifestation of human dignity. The scholastic philosopher and the Catholic theologian recognize freedom, the source of liberty, as a dynamic, liberating creative human power. Freedom in action is the expression of the power of the will that is transcendent; it is the self-affirmation of a human being who, while neither isolated nor completely balanced, yet is responsible and rational and is of intrinsic value by virtue of his or her own nature.

The person who is free has limitations of particular objectives and rarely ever can choose these objectives in such a way that they complement each other perfectly; therefore, there is a lack of perfect balance in life. Freedom is both limited and developed in depth through recognizing the rights of others. When a person does not recognize and concede the rights of others, injustice and license result.

For example, a husband or wife who ignores the rights and desires of one's spouse creates tension, unhappiness, and often divorce. A student who cheats is guilty not only of lying but of an act of injustice to a fellow student who will be graded lower on the scale because of the cheating. A person who does not pay taxes places a greater burden on those who do. The country is true when one makes decisions for the common good.

Since such a person recognizes the good in others, which is the bond he or she shares with them, he or she is never completely isolated or completely alone. As I indicated previously, freedom is a rational faculty, a rational power in action, for the will can never make a particular choice until the intellect presents the possible good. Therefore, in technical language the term "rational faculty" has a specific meaning. We read in the Gospel of St. John: "And you shall know the truth and the truth shall make you free."

In the self-realization that freedom brings, each person can achieve an insight into reality and learn to live in a world that is real though limited. Through this intellectual insight, one is aware that a particular limited good will not completely fulfill the objective of one's being or one's desire for happiness. For example, even in an ideal marriage a husband and wife need space. Each need friendship and companionship with others. Each need quite time. Each relationship can offer an opportunity of personal growth and development. Recognizing the limitation when a particular good is attained, one does not let it dominate but continues to seek that which is greater, that which will lead one closer to a knowledge of God and the purpose of life. Courage in consistently choosing good which is in conformity with human nature enables each person to recognize personal dignity and become a person of integrity.

When a person makes a judgment on a false premise, or when a unit of society forms a policy on the basis of an erroneous philosophy, they are not living in the real world to the extent that their affirmation or negation does not correspond to reality and disorder results.

Any number of illustrations could be offered but I limit myself to two. For example, a person for any number of motives tells a group a deliberate lie. From that moment on there is a limitation of relationships and conversations. The person who lied needs to remember the nature of the lie and the persons who were present or suffer the loss of confidence or reputation. Or, in business if profit is the only objective the rights of the employees, and often the general public, suffers injustices.

A judgment should always be a mental pronouncement about reality, and as such it possesses truth. Therefore, when a premise or a conclusion is derived only from assumptions rather than reality, a lack of self-realization, an isolation from others occurs and a withdrawal from the real world takes place. The individual is despoiled and the group is living on the level of a dialectic. A possible example would be the dialectic of Marx and Engels. They speak of rights and liberty but their understanding is totally different of the understanding of the western world whose philosophy traditionally rests on the acceptance of the spiritual nature of the human person.

Absolute freedom can belong only to God. Only God has the supremacy of intellect capable of recognizing absolute good. Therefore, to consider human freedom as absolute is arrant nonsense. The human intellect is capable of recognizing and understanding only limited good. While this is evidence of human freedom, it also evidences human imperfection. Since the followers of extreme liberalism deny the existence of any divine authority and proclaim that every man is a law unto himself, an ethical system under this guise of liberty quickly degenerates into license; the individual and the state are thereby seriously harmed. The real distinction between what is good and evil, what is true and false, is destroyed; for in this system they exist not in their real nature but in the opinion and judgment of the individual. A legal philosophy which follows this hypothesis will place the individual and the minority at the mercy of the majority; then we have morality by vote. The same holds true for a dictatorship. We of the United States have not accepted as a political philosophy either the extremes of liberalism or materialism. However, we have been adversely influenced by secularism.

In addition to its effect on society as a whole, secularism in its various forms, dominating political and social thought, influences the judgments of individuals in their private lives. When judgments divorced from spiritual and moral values are made, an isolation from one's neighbors results, because then the bond of unity among persons, which is the mutual acceptance of ideas and ideals, exists only as a dialectic. To the extent that a person shares with another transcendental values, he or she is united. To the extent that one does not share or recognize common values, discord often prevails. Though there is an increasing concern for the disorder and unhappiness in the lives of our contemporaries, the content of thought is so dominated by secularism that the source of spiritual values (i.e., the soul of man and divine providence) is often considered irrelevant.

Secularists are so impressed by the obvious fact that both social institutions and moral codes are located in individual minds that they incorrectly conclude that they are purely subjective. Such secularists fail to realize that the mind recognizes a moral code because the object of the intellect is truth, and the object of the will is goodness and happiness. This moral code, existing independently of the individual, is the bond that can and should unite every unit of society in seeking the purpose of their personal and collective existence (i.e., the Ten Commandments, the theological and moral virtues and the Beatitudes.)

Christian philosophy recognizes freedom as experiential datum—i.e., universal personal experiences. A true philosophy does not confuse contingency and freedom. While contingency is the condition of any dependent being, freedom is the result of rational action. Catholic theology recognizes that the ultimate governing power in life is free will. The exercise of free will is limited by a person's capacity for knowledge, by the ability to seek good, and by the consequence of original sin. Yet, aided by divine grace, each person has the power to control his or her conscious life, and to that extent is responsible for happiness here and, under God's providence, ultimately in eternity. In fact, herein lies true dignity. The revealed truth that each person is made in the likeness of God surely is manifest in his controlled activities more than in any other phase of conscious life. All of us have the ability of self-direction, to control relationships with others, to formulate judgments, and thus to effect decisions. Through these activities we recognize that he or she possesses character; is honest, truthful, loyal; is a person of integrity. This self-direction, in the final analysis, has at its source the unselfishness that comes from love.

However, we cannot conclude from this that every act is free; only a conscious deliberate act of the will is free. While the power of human freedom is effective on many levels, it also is restricted by environment and by biological and spiritual heritage. The exercise of freedom also is affected in many ways by former free decisions and by previous conduct and habits. Therefore, freedom is expressed in many degrees, for knowledge and goodness are always limited by participation in reality that can be understood and in ideals that can be possessed. Each person grows day by day through insight into reality, and matures through possession of created good that is recognized as coming from the creative and providential love of God.

Free will is a gift coming from the creative bounty of God Who created each of us to His likeness by calling us into existence through a spiritual immortal soul. The highest level of freedom—i.e., free will properly exercised — that one can attain in this world is accomplished through union with God in the virtue of charity. In this virtue one can attain some detachment from the limitations of human desires. For this reason, there is present in a person a true spiritual grasp of reality and a consistent disposition towards supernatural and eternal good. St. Paul tells us that "we are free in charity, because we are then patient and kind, not envious or proud; that we are not too concerned with our rights, and we do not brood over our injuries." We have the freedom of the children of God. I hope St. Paul is describing you and me. He is if we can live in a relaxed manner with our conscience, which will be considered in the next chapter.

Chapter IV

Conscience

Remember the question the rich young man asked Christ: "Teacher, what must I do to enter eternal life?" We have considered free will, freedom, and liberty. We addressed the questions: Who are we? What kind of person am I? What kind of person am I called to be?

Of necessity the answers to these questions focus on our relations and responsibility to God and to our brothers and sisters in this world. Each decision we make has both personal and communal effects. How we choose right from wrong, good from bad, and penetrate the confusions in life is determined by the human expression of freedom that we call conscience. We are never alone in making these decisions. Remember Christ's promise: "Lo, I am with you always, even to the end of the world" (Matthew 28:20).

Conscience is inherent in the human faculty to search, reason, and choose. It involves a process of reflection, discernment, discussion, discovery, and analysis. Let me share with you my own understanding and appreciation of conscience. Possibly it might seem strange to you that I begin our consideration of conscience with a quotation from one of the foremost proponents of a specific school of psychology, known as depth psychology, Carl Jung. As Dr. Karl Menninger notes in his book *What Happened to Sin?*, Dr. Jung wrote:

During the past thirty years, people from all the civilized countries of the earth have consulted me. I have treated many hundreds of patients, the larger number being Protestants, a small number of Jews and not more than five or six believing Catholics. Among all my patients in the second half of life—that is to say, over thirty-five—there has not been one whose problem in the last resort was not of finding a religious outlook on life. It is safe to say that every one of them fell ill because he had lost that which the living religions of every age have given to their followers, and none of them has been really healed who did not regain his religious outlook.

In our secular society, many have lost the unifying principle or bond rooted in a responsibility to God and the fundamental respect for the dignity and rights of one's neighbor. Unless people possess a unifying bond of values and recognize fundamental rights that are deeper than day-to-day relationships, they will not transcend themselves to reach out to others, and therefore will not be able to work together for the common good.

While we in the United States do not have a unified society, we still have a legal structure in the Constitution that retains some of its original vision, and, if accepted, also is a source for unity. The Constitution of the United States is one of the great documents in the world because it expresses so many truths deduced from the social nature of human beings, and because it was accepted in that light by the society which produced it. But unless the people of this country retain that grasp of reality, even the Constitution can be explained away. The foundation for this bond, which is in the nature of each person, is deeper than even the best of constitutional guarantees.

In order to understand the dignity of each person and social relationships, one must seek out the purpose of life. Human nature is made for love and happiness in this world, with the goal of eternal happiness. When a person is separated from God, he or she has no possibility for permanent happiness or continued union with others or even an integration of their own personality.

We recognize the inherent danger of division that comes from opposing judgments on fundamental values. How does this decision affect us individually? Do we have a consciousness in our daily lives of the presence of God? Do we have a consciousness in our daily lives of the importance of our being, the dignity of ourselves as individuals, or do we just drift along with the forces we are involved in, or the work habits of our daily life? Does our work become an end in itself or, on the contrary, does everything we do have a dignity because we realize the sustaining providence of God? Do we really possess a sufficient knowledge of God's revelation (eternal reality) or are we just repeating something we have heard? Have we made revealed truth our own? In any discussion with our peers, not with a philosopher or a theologian, but with a person of our own background, do we convey an understanding of God's love and God's revelation? Can we evaluate everything we do in relationship with God?

Only through this evaluation can we attain peace and personal security. Knowledge of God and His relationship to us must become personal, not merely something we have read. In other words, revealed truths must become internalized to the extent that these truths are the motivating force of our judgments and love.

Mature knowledge that follows with its insight into reality and grasp of first principles in thought process brings to a person an intellectual security. He or she is then in a position to evaluate data and social experience and thus recognize values, and know who he or she is and why he or she exists.

The foundation for this security is the love of God and the

love of others because they are made to the likeness of God. Personal integrity that flows both from the love of God and of others is the only means possible of finding lasting peace. For a person to possess love, he or she must have an insight into that which is good. Goodness attracts love. To be attracted to that which is good, obviously one has to be able to recognize that which is good. To recognize that which is good, a person has to understand the nature and the order of life. He or she must accept the mystery of God before living within the love of God.

Each person is a created being called into existence by God, and therefore possesses a spiritual quality flowing from God's eternal love. In this light, everyone can be loved. Christ commented on this fact by saying that even the pagans can love those to whom they are attracted, but a Christian must love all people. Christ even went further than this: "Love your enemies." "Be good to those who hate you and pray for those who persecute you." Christ offers a strong love, a supernatural and unselfish love, not the weak, sentimental, mushy concentration on approval that we often encounter in the travesty of culture in modern music and soap operas. (Please don't confuse "loving" with "liking." Let me explain: We like only those who we admire for the way they live. In accepting the love of Christ, we love a person that they in turn might accept the redemptive love of Christ. That is, we seek that which is good for them.)

Love is not affection, love is not attraction or compassion, love is not an emotional reaction to something or someone present to us. Love is a realization that God created each one of us to find happiness, and that every living person has a right to happiness. Because of your love of God, you seek to bring this love to others, whether you are attracted to them or not. This is what will enable any individual to be detached somewhat from the problems in life. One is not thrown off balance because one can always love. If one possesses the strength of this love, he or she influences the limited society wherein he or she moves. If he or she has not reached out to others, he or she really does not love. If every Christian really loved God and his neighbor, as we are capable of loving through the gift of sanctifying grace, the entire world eventually would have the opportunity to hear the Gospel proclaimed. But we have not responded as we could, and thus we limit the growth of the love of God on earth. But it is still possible, even now, in our own unit of society, to influence the segment of society in which we move, to find peace ourselves, and, in so finding peace, to bring it to others. We can do this, for the nature of love is diffusive. By this I mean it is impossible to love unless I love someone and share that love.

The motivating force of love is both the source and catalyst necessary to the accomplishment of unity and harmony in society. If we are not capable of giving of ourselves, a vacuum exists in our lives, and that vacuum will be filled by material and transient goals and pleasures. Unless there is a realistic approach to life on the level of love, change or conversion will not be accomplished. Do we realize that the starting point must be a deep understanding of the purpose of life and the spiritual potential of each person?

If a person's thoughts are centered in God, the realization of personal dignity follows. Through faith we then know that we were created to the likeness of God. Recognizing our limitation as one who is created, we realize that we are sustained in existence by God's providential concern. Our personal grace, strength and happiness will be in ratio to our acceptance of the love and providence of God. We notice a tendency to anxiety, a tendency to excess in the passions, a tendency to give in to the appetites, a tendency to follow the line of least resistance, a tendency to exaggerate our own importance; we notice that we must battle the key sin of the world—pride. We can succeed in the journey through life—not perfectly, but by the grace of God we realize personal identity and can direct our efforts together toward the pursuit of happiness.

If we accept the truth that God called us into existence, we also will accept that personal dignity and responsibility come from that gift of life. Rights, duties and freedom come from the nature that God gave us. We all have them simply because we are human, not because of our level of intelligence, background, contributions to society, race, class or nationality. Each person is both sacred and social by nature.

The difficulty is that as individuals and as co-responsible members of society we do not live up to the human potential that is ours that came both from creation and redemption. We sadly acknowledge the struggle of personal sin expressed in choice and action, together with the social consequences of sin in the structures of human communities.

Sin exists not in action, but in the will, that is, choosing to misuse God's gifts, and in so doing rejecting a love relationship with God. You may ask: How do I know that I am committing sin? How do I recognize that I am disordering my relationship with God? The answers are found in an informed conscience. We have the Ten Commandments; we have the "Sermon on the Mount"; we have the virtues taught by Christ throughout His public life. We have the Church established by Christ and guided by the Holy Spirit.

Yet, in the final analysis we are the ones that must make the judgment. We have our conscience. But conscience is not something outside or inside of us saying, "Yes, you can," or "no, you can't" do something. Conscience is a judgment that each person makes from knowledge of revelation and the natural law. Each time we make a judgment about something we are about to do, and whether that something is good or bad, our conscience is acting.

I do not think anyone will question the fact that evil exists in the world. Sometimes it is not easy to discern what is evil—because of our culture, because of our own hang-ups, because of the ambiguity of our lives. Therefore, throughout our lives we continue to work towards an informed conscience. To accomplish this, we are not alone. Christ instituted the Church to proclaim His mission, to teach eternal truths that He revealed. Sometimes, however, we forget that Christ revealed truths in principles in a particular culture of history, under existing circumstances of that age; but the truths He revealed, while eternal, must be translated in succeeding cultures and varied languages from a point of reference of where people are today. What Christ revealed does not change, but there is no question that we change and must make concrete the revelation of Christ in our lives.

Through baptism and confirmation Christians belong to the faith community we call the Church. The Holy Spirit works in the Church in every generation, but not every person or every generation responds to the Holy Spirit. While we identify with the Church and her teaching, the Church cannot make our decisions for us. No one (or even the Church, established by Christ to proclaim His teaching) can move into the life of anyone and make his or her decisions; it is unreal and unfair to ask someone to make a moral judgment for a mature Christian.

Christian maturity is possible for anyone whose gifts of intellect and will are normal and active, and therefore responsible. Being a Christian is not something like putting on or taking off a coat; it is not something superficial or accidental to our psyche or our human personality. When we are baptized, we enter a covenant relationship with God, and this covenant relationship is consummated wherever love is offered and accepted.

Because we are human and limited and also are social beings, we must live and depend on each other. To accomplish this, we need law (divine law and sometimes human law) to make a covenant relationship realistic in life. Because of this need for law, we can never move away from it. Moral law facilitates the living out of this relationship of God and neighbor. It is necessary for us to study, to pray, to listen, so that we can discern what God would have us do. Therefore, we cannot just step away, and off the top of our head make decisions. We certainly need more depth. Each and every day, each one of us must accept the responsibility of integrating the data offered through experience and faith. This is vital and personal in the total process of moral decision-making.

It is on this level that we speak of conscience. We must always remember who we are. We are the Church, a community of faith, and we are individuals within the Church, and each of us has received an invitation and has the obligation to respond to the Holy Spirit and form our own conscience.

Let me recall to you that the role of the conscience is that of a judge, not a teacher; that conscience does not teach what is good or evil, nor does it create good or evil. It weighs accumulated knowledge and principles, makes a judgment in very concrete, not theoretical situations—the concrete situations of our lives.

In most instances, one who accepts the gift of grace and uses his or her native talents can arrive at good sound judgment with moral certitude. Absolute certainty in complex moral matters is seldom possible. Moral certitude is the norm for practically all judgments in practically all fields of knowledge. Because of this reality, certainly there is a possibility for legitimate disagreement. In making decisions that seriously affect our lives, we thank God for the gift of faith that brings to us clear, not childlike, security. With this security, we accept responsibility for those committed to our care with fidelity in all human relationships.

It is in accepting the responsibility for moral decision-making that each person activates the uniquely human qualities of intelligence and free will which are the great gifts of God. The power to develop and shape the future, to determine the course of individual and communal human existence, is an awesome one. The Christian faces the challenge with grace and faith: that God does care about the individual and the world; and that with the enduring hope and promise of God to be always with us, the Church mediates that faith and that hope.

A well-formed and honest human conscience allows the Christian to make moral decisions boldly and responsibly. Yet even a conscience so formed and so exercised admits the risk of error. We are going to make mistakes, and we will risk error; but, please God, we will so live that sin will not be an option in our lives. We can make a mistake without sin. Sin is the only thing in the world that ruptures our relationship with God. Ultimately, for a mature person, sin is the only thing that can bring unhappiness.

Now I am not equating sadness with unhappiness. We can be sad and very good and moral. We can be disillusioned and good and moral. We can fail in various projects and be good and moral. Happiness ultimately is a relationship with God and neighbor. This relationship frees us to relate in harmony with other people, even though because of human weakness and sin harmony does not always result.

Lumen Gentium of Vatican II treats our ultimate union with God in this, our period of salvation history. The Council Fathers stated explicitly that Scripture teaches that God wills the salvation, the eternal happiness, of all persons. But there is always the second movement to this symphony of love—i.e., that a person cannot be saved without himself or without herself. Every person must turn freely to God. For us who believe in an order over and above that of the temporal and the temporary, this turning to God and the acceptance of His loving Will, is called an act of faith. It is a free decision of a person who accepts as true that God has spoken to us. Scripture tells us that, in former times, in fragmentary and varied fashions God has spoken through the prophets; but in this final age, He has spoken to us in His Son.

St. Paul tells us that we must "put on the mind of Christ." To put on the mind of Christ, we need time for silence and reflection in our lives. Can any one of us say that "I do not have the time"? Time is also a gift of God, from the moment when we were conceived in our mother's womb until the moment of our death when we will have made the ultimate judgment of our relationship with God.

We pray that this ultimate judgment will be a normal, peaceful and happy culmination of our lifelong relationship with Jesus the Risen Christ. We know from Jesus the foundation of morality is the total commitment to a single goal in life, to enter into God's reign—the communion of God's own life. Remember as we read in the Gospel according to St. John Christ revealed: "I have given them [my disciples] the glory you have given Me that they may be one as We are one—I living in them, You living in Me, that their unity may be complete" (John 17:22).

This relationship with Christ is a mystery we will never fully understand in this life. However, by analogy from our experience of a spiritual relationship with others we will also recognize a spiritual relationship with God. In the next chapter we will explore this spiritual reality.

Chapter V

❧

The Natural
to the
Supernatural

The character and personality of everyone born into this world (and specifically of every Christian) is the result of free decisions in the use of natural talents infused with the redemptive love of Christ. How does this take place? In the generic sense, the growth process is the same for everyone; yet each person is unique and no two people are exactly alike. Each of us is conscious of our own being and of the personal ability to direct our lives. No two people have exactly the same experiences, the same level of gifts, or are affected in the same manner by pressure. Therefore, when we discuss free will, natural gifts and the vital presence of God, each one of us must look to ourselves, not someone else, to discover the kind of person we are.

In the order of creation, every person is granted an inherent dignity that is native or natural to human existence. Therefore everyone, in the order of nature, should experience this dignity because he and she has been created in the likeness of God, possessing a spiritual soul, with a capacity for knowledge and love. This is so fundamental and basic that the classical definition that separates the human from the animal is: "a spiritual being who can know and love."

Often in common parlance the terms "spiritual" and "supernatural" are used interchangeably. This is a mistake. In the context of philosophy and theology, that which is spiritual is considered as non-material (i.e., the soul, ideals, choice, etc., are not physical or material); the supernatural is that which pertains to God. It is through a natural use of these spiritual powers that man transcends himself. Through the medium of this transcendency, everyone is capable of attaining knowledge, even though limited, and to that extent a person can possess an insight into reality.

First, as an intellectual being he or she can recognize the order in the created world and that which is good or bad, both in the generic sense and with personal realization. Second, through the power of free will, each person has the ability to choose that which is good, and in its possession can attain a degree of happiness. Through the power of choice, which controls even the forces of passion and the tendencies of habit, one evidences a power transcending purely biological urges. For example, a person is a being capable of self-knowledge, and can also look to the future and weigh in advance possibilities, advantages and disadvantages. Aware of this potential, every person of integrity accepts the responsibility for actions resulting from decision and choice. The possession of integrity is not something easily attained or lightly considered, it is a virtue that requires complete honesty and the courage to live up to that which one believes.

Yet the natural limitations of our own ability and the finite nature of the world in which we live limits our potential. If we are going to find lasting happiness, peace and security, it must be in God. We must be saved from our sins. But as Archbishop Fulton Sheen stated in a sermon a number of years ago: "We want to be saved, but not from our sins." I do not think he was being sarcastic.

We want to be saved from poverty, from unhappiness, from ignorance, but do we really want to be saved from our sins? Do we really ask to have control over our pride? Do we really seek to have control over our appetites, to possess the ability to order every faculty of our being to God? Do we really want to do the will of God, or do we want to be saved only the unpleasantness that follows disorder in the world? Are we limited to seeking comfort? But how much are we willing, really, to put forth for our quest of goodness and happiness? We are probably willing to serve on different committees in our church and in our city. We would even be willing to give up a couple of evenings a week if it would not interfere too much with our more or less accepted routine in life; but are we really willing to give of ourselves in the spirit of St. Paul: "I live now, not I but Christ lives in me"? Are we willing in our life to choose freely what God wants us to do and accept it?

A moral theologian might call this a fundamental option, but it is really more than that. Through the gift of faith and the power of grace, we are disposed by God to truly commit ourselves to a consistent journey through life to heaven. The key question is: Are we ready to do this? Often we are not completely willing to do the will of God. We make all kinds of reservations along the line. We want to go part way and we are afraid of making a commitment because we are afraid of what we might be asked to do. We are afraid of losing control.

So for example, would you agree with me that this fear is most evident in the fear of death? Most men and women of faith are not afraid of dying. They have confidence in God's mercy and love. Their fear seems to rest on moving from one level of existence wherein they are in control to the unknown and different mode of existence.

We are seeking personal security and, in fact, it is impossible for a person to live without seeking the security of his or her being. Everyone seeks financial security, and everyone seeks in marriage the security of conjugal love. A happily married person recognizes that financial security is as nothing compared to the security of conjugal love. The security of friendship is likewise much deeper than financial security. It transcends anything material.

But, even though the security of human love is vital, it is

not even remotely comparable to the security of being. This concept is basic and fundamental because it is founded in a realization that each person possesses an individuality as a spiritual being, separate and apart from all others, a dignity realized in its source—God's eternal personal love. Those lacking this security are never free of the fear of despair. We are not going to be here very long; perhaps another ten or thirty—or possibly fifty—years or so. What is this life all about? We are going to die; this is a reality. Why were we born? We often go back to the basic questions. Why are we living? What is the meaning and purpose of life? Are we convinced of an immortal soul? Is there life after death? What is the source and nature of this life? Until these questions are answered with reasonable certitude, anything we do in life is inadequate and incomplete; we feel a lack of fulfillment that prevents even the reasonable peace that we hope to have in this world. Such peace can be accomplished only through faith. We can have adequate knowledge and yet be miserable, because we do not have love and do not commit ourselves to a life of virtue. We need a commitment to faith and charity.

Therefore, we must have a friendship beyond the human—that is, a friendship with God. Considering the nature of friendship and love, a human being—a creature totally dependent for existence—would not have hoped to use the term "friendship" in relationship to God, if God the Son had not come into the world, shared our life, and invited us to share His. Through revelation, we know that God has raised us to the possibility of knowing and possessing Him as He is in Himself. As the Apostle St. John tells us: "Dearly beloved, we are now the sons of God; and it has not yet appeared what we shall be. We know that when He shall appear, we shall be like to Him because we shall see Him as He is" (1 John 3:2).

Friendship does not limit God, for in divine causality

friendship is effective, creative; God loves us that He might make us good—i.e., live in harmony with His creative and redemptive love. We, in turn, receive the friendship and thus move and act with a supernatural power. Supernatural here is understood as the presence of God in the created order which, though distinct from God, is nevertheless related to God. Supernatural in the full and proper sense relates to God in His own existence, in the Holy Trinity and for us in the Beatific Vision.

An understanding of man's share in the supernatural life challenges the deepest insight of the human intellect. How can God, an infinite, eternal, spiritual Being, share His life with a limited, temporal, even though spiritual, creature? Though this is a great mystery, we approach an answer to this question through an understanding of our own natural spiritual power and growth. We recognize our native ability to transcend time and the physical and material things and creatures of this world. We approach some understanding through an analogy of adoption. All analogies are inadequate, but this is the only method available to the human intellect. Using the method with which we are so familiar, we can begin to have an insight into this divine relationship.

Previous chapters have already considered the fact that any permanent union or bond among persons is spiritual in nature. Any quality that is spiritual is transcendent and can be shared without loss. For example, a teacher conducting a class, or a lecturer addressing an audience, conveys knowledge to those assembled without the loss of knowledge that is his. His ideas can become their ideas because of the natural spiritual capacity to make a concept or an idea one's own. The idea becomes an integral part of a person's intellectual life and background. He has the ability and power to use this knowledge to grow intellectually to gain other insights into the created world. Each person in the group simultaneously shares these ideas and possesses these powers.

We can apply a similar analogy to the possession and sharing of love. We have defined love as the constant effective desire to bring good to another. This spiritual capacity to forget one's self in seeking the goodness and happiness of another brings about a detachment from particular things and a further forgetfulness of self. This, in turn, produces a greater capacity for personal love and happiness. When one gives love and shares love, not only does he or she not lose, but he or she actually gains in the sharing.

Through an understanding of the thought process and a realization of the capacity to give and receive love without loss, we recognize the natural spiritual potential of growth and development for each person. However, this still does not explain how a finite, limited human being is able to share the life of the infinitely perfect God. Through revelation we know that grace becomes the principle of divine life in us; that through grace people attain the dignity of adopted sons and daughters of God.

Our knowledge of human generation and gaining children through adoption will be a definite help. Human generation is the result of the natural processes in the drive towards the propagation of the species and the preservation of family bonds and inheritance. A spiritual bond obviously is necessary to bring about a family unit; the adopted child is united to his or her adoptive parents through the spiritual bond of knowledge and love as is the child of conception and birth from parental intercourse.

In divine adoption, the relationship is constant and thus the difference between divine and human adoption is profound. In human adoption there is a spiritual and legal bond, but the bond does not penetrate the physical nature of the one adopted. He or she remains the natural child with the physical characteristics of the original parents. The natural powers of the adopted child spring from his natural parents as immediate, efficient causes; whereas in divine adoption in both human existence and grace—the principle of divine life—come from God as the source and efficient cause. Thus, without changing the essential order of nature, grace penetrates the very depth of the human soul, the divine love shared becomes our love, and we become truly children of God. A child of the natural order, though sharing from the life of his father and mother, is separate from them. We, though sharing the divine life while having our own personality and being, are not separate from God. Although God is infinite and self-existent, our sharing in the divine life is limited by our finite nature. We are not gods. Yet, since it is the divine life and power that transforms our soul, we have a supernatural power, knowledge and love, and our nature is elevated. A German theologian expressed the character of this transformation as follows:

> This change cannot make a new human nature, for it would destroy the unity of a person who already possesses a complete nature. Nor can it mean that the divine nature becomes the intrinsic vital principle of our acts, for this would obscure the distinction between Creator and creature. If this intrinsic change in the sanctified soul cannot be a new substance nor God Himself, it must be an accident in the soul. We can best classify it among the accidents as a habit. It is a habit which raises nature and underlies the virtues. The virtues, in turn, raise the faculties so they can perform supernatural acts.

Through this supernatural elevation of the soul, each person has a new life, a new power, a new source of action that will enable him one day to possess and love God as He exists in Himself. St. Peter in his Second Epistle tells us: "He has given us most great and precious promises: that by these you may be made partakers of the divine nature: flying the corruption of that concupiscence which is in the world" (2 Peter 1:4).

Human nature is raised to the dignity of acting with a divine power. We begin to understand the nature of holiness when we see that our actions are not merely ethical (i.e., according to the nature and rights of a human being), but supernatural, because they are directed to the source of all nature and rights—God Himself. Thus a person possessing the divine life sees and chooses everything in relation to God. He or she does not negate nor neglect the good in the world but correlates that good with its source. One is not thrown off balance nor blocked by the evil in this world, but rises above this disorder in the hope that the essential good of one's very existence might be redirected to God. Only in this light can we understand the command of Christ: "Love your enemies, do good to them that hate you, pray for them who persecute you."

One who lives a supernatural life does not deny the evil in the world, but recognizes it and is not controlled by the evil encountered. While experiencing a sadness in the evil of others, and recognizing the disorder in their relationship to God, it is possible to attain an objectivity that enables one to pray for those responsible for evil, because of the personal peace experienced that is inherent in the order of God's creative and shared love.

Evil, which came into the world through original sin and its rejection of the supernatural, is contained by the redemption of Christ and the restoration of man to the supernatural order. An essential understanding of the Incarnation includes this restoration of the supernatural. Christ the God-Man is the redeemer, mediator and brother of mankind. St. Paul reiterates this throughout his epistles. "He has graced us in His beloved Son." He has resolved "to re-establish all things," "to gather together all things under one head." In his Epistle to the Galatians, St. Paul also clearly states: "God sent His Son that we might receive the adoption of sons."

The life which we are to have abundantly, of which St. Paul and St. John speak, introduces us to the second aspect of the relationship of the soul with God. This comes with the actual indwelling of the Holy Spirit and thus of the Holy Trinity. Through the presence of the Holy Trinity, people have the ability to love God even in His creatures which came into being through God's loving gift of self. This power to love is effected through the presence of sanctifying grace. The soul has an immediate relationship with God, and through this relationship or habit, God becomes the object of thought and love. We should again recognize that this involves no change in God, since the divine nature is spiritual and absolutely transcendent. The change comes to man who, though already created as a spiritual being, is united to God through the vital principle of supernatural love—i.e., a share of the redemptive love of Christ.

A realization of the love of God expressed in the hypostatic union offers a true approach in understanding of the supernatural. God the Son, eternally existing in His divine nature, became man in the order of time by taking a human nature for Himself. Revelation clearly teaches that Jesus Christ is a divine person with a human nature. This union of the divine and human in the person of Christ serves as the redemptive bridge between God and all people. Christ the divine person who possesses heaven shares our human nature that we, in union with Him, might have a share of the divine life. The same infinite power that creates human nature with its spiritual capacity shares sanctifying grace with the supernatural capacity to know and love God.

The transient, limited good that we encounter in the

things of the world cannot ever fully satisfy a person's craving for happiness. The disorder, inordinate attraction and misuse of the pleasures of the world can prevent one from attaining even the happiness possible in the order of nature and time. Thus we begin to recognize the purpose of the Incarnation: the reparation for the injustice offered to the infinite majesty of God through sin and the redemption of the human race from this rejection of God. The Holy Trinity has granted to each person a distinct and particular relation with each of the Divine Persons. We are children of the Father, adopted sons and daughters; we are brothers and sisters of Christ, sharing His divine life; we are co-workers with the Holy Spirit, moving under His guidance with the power of divine love.

One could think that it is the height of presumption to claim that we are adopted children of God and brothers and sisters of Christ. For that reason let us look to Sacred Scripture and the great Councils of the Church in the next chapter.

Chapter VI

Grace

S t. Paul tells us in his Letter to the Ephesians that everyone who believes in Christ has a relationship with Him. He writes:

> Praised be the God and father of our Lord Jesus Christ, who has bestowed on us in Christ every spiritual blessing in the heavens! God chose us in him before the world began, to be holy and blameless in his sight, to be full of love; he likewise predestined us through Christ Jesus to be his adopted sons—such was his will and pleasure—that all might praise the glorious favor he had bestowed on us in his beloved.
>
> It is Christ and through his blood that we have been redeemed and our sins forgiven, so immeasurably generous is God's favor to us. God has given us the wisdom to understand fully the mystery, the plan he was pleased to decree in Christ, to be carried out in the fullness of time: namely, to bring all things in the heavens and on earth into one under Christ's headship. (Ephesians 1: 3-10)

Down through the centuries Christians have identified this relationship with Christ as the gift of grace. Unconsciously when we speak of grace, we Catholics and other Christians often think of the gift of grace beginning with the passion and death of Christ. Others possibly having a broader knowledge of Sacred Scripture think in terms of grace possibly beginning with the call of Abraham, down through Moses and Jewish history, until the fulfillment in the birth of Our Lord. These concepts, even though rooted in a positive way in the redemptive love of Jesus Christ, limit the love of God through possibly one-and-a-half million years that evidence indicates intelligent life has existed in this world. Since God called each person into existence and granted to everyone a spiritual soul wherein each one could be united with God, limiting God's love relationship to Judeo-Christian history would contradict the reality and truth that God is love.

The Fathers of the Second Vatican Council stated so very clearly that each and every one of us is a member of the human family, and that relationship is not limited to the ten thousand years of recorded human history, but includes every person from the beginning of time. I would suggest that the history of grace and the history of salvation coincide with the history of human beings in this world. The coming of Our Lord, God the Son, into the world is the culmination of the sharing of God's love at a period in time when Divine Providence chose to move in human history in such a manner that people could accept the bonding of faith and love and therefore form a faith community that is even deeper than a human family.

The occasion and circumstances wherein God, in his love, moved into the lives of people during the continuum of these million years we do not know, and there is no need for us to know. We do know, however, that the most primitive people of pre-historic ages are loved by God equally as the most sophisticated, and each person is granted the necessary spiritual support to accomplish the purpose of life.

In an introduction to Teilhard de Chardin's incisive work, *The Appearance of Man*, Robert Francoeur tries to relate our long past to our present history. He says: "Let us propose a comparison of humankind's history with a calendar year in which one day equals four thousand years of human history. In that approach, six thousand to ten thousand years of which we have records are nestled in the last two days of our year...Socrates, Plato, and Aristotle (the ancient Greek philosophers) would have been born on December 31. The final hour of December 31 from 11 p.m. to midnight would embrace all of the nineteenth and twentieth centuries." This comparison boggles the mind, but anyone who has received the gift of faith and has willingly accepted and lives within the love of God that He has shared with us could not possibly limit the love of God to those people who have lived since the time of Abraham or within the ten thousand years of recorded history.

With this speculative analogy of time and love in God's creation, I will begin this discussion of grace with four quotations; one each from St. John, St. Paul, Father Karl Rahner, and St. Augustine, respectively.

"God so loved the world that He gave His only Son, that whoever believes in Him should not perish but have eternal life" (John 3:16).

"When the perfect comes, the imperfect will pass away...Now we see in a mirror dimly, but then face to face. Now I know in part, but then I shall know even as I am known" (from 1 Corinthians 13:10, 12—we will know God as God knows us).

"God Himself as the abiding and holy mystery, as the incomprehensible ground of man's transcendent existence, is not only the God of infinite distance, but also wants to be the God of absolute closeness, in true self-communication, and is present in this way in the spiritual depths of our existence as well as the concreteness of our corporeal history" (from *Foundations*, p. 137—even in this life, we not only can transcend the physical, material and temporal, but also can transcend ourselves).

"Our hearts are longing for you, O Lord, and will

not rest until they rest in You" (St. Augustine).

St. Augustine, writing in the fourth century, articulated the longing for happiness that every person feels. The hope of every person is rooted in the seeking of a total security, a love that lasts and in an unclouded happiness. This longing has never been completely fulfilled, but it stays with us whatever we may do, and sets the tone for every day of our lives. This is true not only for the major goals and hopes of our lives, but also true of the most ordinary details. For example: You would like to have some friends over for dinner. They come, you enjoy each other's company, but after a few hours you are glad when they go home and they, in turn, are glad to leave. This is true in family life, too. You love your grandchildren, but you can take them only in small doses.

Let us consider something much more important and in more depth. You would like to find in marriage the ideal wife, the ideal husband. You almost did and you are happy, but you are glad each day that you have some space for yourself. At retirement time, for most people, this becomes even more important. A husband or wife cannot completely fill the other's need for security and happiness, even though they experience a wonderful married life. No one person or group of persons, no succession of accomplishments or exquisite pleasures can completely fill our needs and our hope for immortality. These pleasant experiences come to an end, they pass; and for the most part we are glad that they do. At the same time, these good experiences bring joy even though they come to an end. In one of Claudel's plays, a woman says: "I am a promise that can never be kept, and that is just my charm."

When we reflect like this we ask ourselves the meaning of life. Since this longing for fulfillment and happiness is inherent and constant in our very being, it is meant to be attained.

We are safe and sure, for this longing is founded on something greater and dearer than anything on earth. It is rooted in God's love that He shares with us. St. Paul tells us in his Letter to the Romans: "God's love has been poured into our hearts, through the Holy Spirit" (Romans 5:5). St. Paul does not mean love given to God, but love from God. Through the love of God in creation and the redemptive love of Christ, we are men and women who love and who are loved—not through merit, but from a divine gift.

This love is what we traditionally call Sanctifying Grace. It is the mystery of our personal relationship with God. Grace is not a thing, not a concept, rather it is the presence of God within us. On God's side, grace is God offering himself, communicating His life, requiring from us love and fidelity. On our human side, grace is offering oneself to God as a person who has been transformed, shaped to Christ and by Christ. Grace is what the early Greek Fathers described as: "God became man to make men Gods." St. Paul reflected in his letters that he had been grasped by the person of Christ. We, like St. Paul, as true Christians accept His forgiveness, participate in His passion, and will experience His resurrection. St. John in his first letter states the eternal conclusion: "When Christ appears, we shall be like Him, for we will see Him as He is" (1 John 3:2).

A Christian accepting the teaching of Christ as expressed by St. Paul and St. John lives according to the dynamics of faith, hope and love, and thus enters into a new life, to become a new person in Christ. This new life, inasmuch as the bonding is the redemptive love of Christ, is always shared with others, and the community of faith (which is the Church) results.

The Catholic tradition in every century has always been insistent that the grace of God is given to us, not to make up something lacking to us as human persons, but as a free gift that elevates us to a new and unmerited level of existence. Hypothetically, we could have a natural end in the created order if grace did not exist. But as we read in Sacred Scripture: "God wills all men to be saved and come to a knowledge of the truth." The real historical order, however, is already permeated with grace, so that the state of nature isolated from God does not exist. In other words, if grace supposes nature, nature in its own way supposes grace. The providence of God sustains us in existence and the redemptive love of Christ (i.e., grace) orients us toward a supernatural end (i.e., the Kingdom of God). By grace we enter into a new relationship of communion with God and we are transformed interiorly by the Spirit of Christ. We should always remember, as stated in the prologue of the Gospel of St. John and in 1 Colossians, that God created us and the world in and through Christ, God the Son, Our Lord Jesus Christ. Theological conclusions drawn from revelation are that we were created, called into existence, to participate in the very life of God through Jesus Christ.

The analysis of grace that I have presented certainly should not rest on my own personal understanding. Therefore, I would like to quote four examples of the official teaching of the Church from the sixth century to the present day:

1. *Second Council of Orange (520)*: "If anyone asserts that by his natural strength he is able to think as is required or choose anything good pertaining to his eternal salvation, or to assent to the saving message of the Gospel without the illumination and inspiration of the Holy Spirit .... he is deceived by the heretical spirit..." (canon 7; see also canons 3-6, 8).

2. *Council of Trent (1547)*: "Thus, not only are we considered just, but we are truly called just and we are just, each one receiving within himself his own justice, according to the measure which 'the Holy Spirit apportions to each one indi-

vidually as He wills' (1 Corinthians 12:11), and according to each one's personal disposition and cooperation" (chapter VII; see the entire "Decree on Justification").

3. *Pope Leo XIII, encyclical letter* Divinum Illud *(1897)*: "...by grace God abides in the just soul as in a temple, in a most intimate and singular manner .... Now this wonderful union, which is properly called indwelling .... is most certainly produced by the divine presence of the [Holy] Trinity: 'We will come to him and make our home with him' (John 14:23); nevertheless it is attributed in a particular manner to the Holy Spirit."

4. *Second Vatican Council, Dogmatic Constitution on the Church (1964)*: "The Spirit dwells in the Church and in the hearts of the faithful as in a temple..." (n.4).

The Catholic theological tradition is grounded first of all in the New Testament's perspective of a Christocentric universe (1 Corinthians 8:6, 15:24-28, 44-49; Romans 8:19-23, 29, 30; Ephesians 1:9-14, 19-23, 3:11; Colossians 1:15-20, 3:4; Philippians 3:21; Hebrews 1: 2-3; John 1:3, 12:32). All creation is oriented toward the covenant between God and the People of God. The Covenant of the Old Testament orients people of all ages toward the New Covenant grounded in the incarnation of the Son of God in Jesus Christ. The human community of the entire world (i.e., this planet earth) in which the human community exists is oriented toward Christ and is sustained by Him. Although hypothetically it could have been otherwise, it in fact has not been otherwise. There is no creation except in view of Christ. There is no covenant except in view of Christ. There is no human existence, therefore, except in view of Christ and of our New Covenant in Christ.

While this theological analysis is essential for conceptual insight, in reality grace (i.e., this loved relationship) is lived on a very personal level. (For example, my mother, who was a beautiful simple person, would have had a difficulty in following abstract theological discussions, yet she lived a life of love and grace far superior to many learned men and women. She understood without qualification that we are human beings called by God into existence, that we are what we are in the sight of God and nothing more—but that this reality is something wonderful.) This gift of grace and love has a vitality and warmth because it is personal. While grace and love are defined and understood in the abstract, they are always shared and experienced in personal relationships. Love in human relationships normally is manifested through the senses; from admiration and desire to concern and compassion. Sometimes love is spontaneous, sometimes it is willed—i.e., it is deliberate. By analogy, while God's love for us would be called spontaneous, our response to the movement of grace is sometimes deliberate. The emotions and senses offer little help. With faith, we respond like St. Paul: "Without God I can do nothing."

Sin is an exercise of human freedom against a person's relationship with God. The gift and presence of grace, however, is not destroyed by sin. The sinner, by God's providence, remains radically open to the possibility of conversion and of forgiveness. If grace were not still available to the sinner, conversion and forgiveness would be impossible. The call of God to conversion and repentance (1 Corinthians 1:9; Galatians 2:20; Romans 8:28-30) would be meaningless unless there were some basis in the human person for responding to the call. Grace supposes even in the sinner the capacity to receive it. As previously stated, this capacity is what Karl Rahner and other Transcendental Thomists call our "limitless openness to being and ultimately to the Absolute," which openness constitutes the human person as "spirit in the world."

Despite human limitations and the disorder and malice of sin, grace always orients and sustains us in our every human experience. Catholic theology from St. Augustine through the teaching of St. Thomas Aquinas through the transcendental theologians of the present century has always recognized an inherent "natural desire" for direct union with God. It is only in the vision of God that the human mind and will can satisfy fully its desire to know and love. No finite reality can satisfy these desires. It is only in the encounter with God, the Absolute, the source of our being and the fount of love, that our deepest spiritual aspirations are fulfilled.

There is no merely natural end of human existence. All creation comes from God and is radically oriented towards God. The history of the world is, at the same time, the history of salvation. We read in the Letter of St. Paul to the Romans: "Indeed the whole created world eagerly awaits the revelation of the sons of God. Creation was made subject to futility not by its own accord, but by Him Who once subjected it; yet not without hope, because the world itself will be freed from slavery to corruption and share in the glorious freedom of the children of God. Yes, we know that all creation groans and is in agony even until now. Not only that, but we ourselves, although we have the Spirit as first fruits, groan inwardly while we await the redemption of our bodies" (Romans 8:19-23).

The Fathers of the Second Vatican Council in their final document echo this teaching of St. Paul: "We recognize in this history of salvation that the whole history of authentic human progress is the struggle for justice, peace, freedom, human rights and so forth is part of the movement of and for the Kingdom of God" (*Gaudium et Spes*).

This also means that human freedom is never apart from grace, because the grace of God is always operative even if rejected through pride or selfishness. When grace is accepted, there is a dynamism of human freedom because it converges not only with the providence of God, but also, as St.

John tells us, literally "with the indwelling" of God Himself.

By self-gift or self-communication of God, we understand simply that God offers Himself to us in unsurpassable proximity; the giver is Himself the gift. God does not merely give us finite gifts, nor merely communicate to us truths about Himself. He offers His presence to us in a manner that surpasses his relationship to us as Creator. This divine self-gift is offered and takes place on a personal level. A full personal relationship with God is established only with one who responds to the divine offer, with at least implicit faith, hope and love. This relationship always begins with God. We love because God first loved us.

Although God's self-communication or indwelling is present throughout our lives, it does not reach its definitive state until our death, since only then is our acceptance or rejection final. Again, let us refer to St. Paul and recognize the difference of our present state and our state of final perfection which we hope to enjoy after death: "When the perfect comes, the imperfect will pass away... Now we see in a mirror dimly, but then face to face. Now I know in part, but then I shall know even as I am known" (1 Corinthians 13:10, 12).

In Father Karl Rahner's treatise on grace, he holds that we do not relate with God as a distant and aloof horizon of mystery, but we experience God in our very person and are transformed by Him. His basic understanding of grace is that grace properly understood is not a finite, created gift separate from God, but the self-communication of God. Grace is not something, it is someone. God does not merely give some indirect share of Himself; rather, in the strict sense of the word, He gives Himself. While God is an absolute mystery, through His self-communication we participate in His life; we are transformed, we become like God without, however, becoming God. Such a transformation is the fulfillment of our deepest human potential and is therefore our salvation.

The essence of being human is being open to the unfath-omable mystery of God. When God draws near to us in grace, God does what no one or nothing else can do: He fills the empty abyss of our hearts with His own unfathomable mystery of being. This gracious self-communication of God becomes fruitful and effective when accepted in faith.

We are never completely human until we accept and experience our relationship with God. Only through faith can we live this relationship. Faith, both human and divine, is our primary source of knowledge and personal growth. In the next chapter I hope together we can explore this reality.

Chapter VII

❧

The Validity
of
Knowledge

The ancient psalmist prayed: "Lord, make me know your ways. Lord, teach me your paths" (Psalm 25). Before we can know what the Lord will have us do, we must first accept our spiritual gifts that are integral to our human nature. God gave us an intellect that, in the order of nature, must always seek truth, and a free will to strive for that which is good. So now we can ask: How do we think clearly? How do we recognize truth? The cynic or skeptic through rationalization would question even the possibility of attaining truth. Even Pilate, before he sentenced Jesus to death, asked the question: "What is truth?"

We need to think clearly so we can choose properly in order to direct our lives to fulfillment and happiness. Ultimately, we will not make the right decisions unless we accept the gift of love from God that enables us to rise above our limitations and seek the good for everyone with whom we live, work and recreate. We have considered these human possibilities when we studied free will and grace. Now we will explore the thought process in order to discover the validity of human knowledge.

Today, we live in a world that is growing both at the same time ever closer and yet farther apart. On the one hand, there are astonishing new technologies for communication and travel; on the other hand, as persons and communities, we seem to be more separate and isolated. We can dial a call direct to another continent. On television we daily follow the political changes in Eastern Europe, and the devastation and sad conditions in the Middle East and the ethnic battles in what was Yugoslavia. We have information about the different planets in our solar system from information sent by our rocket-propelled laboratories. Yet, at the same time, we as a people in these United States and the world community do not think together about fundamental values in this life and the purpose of our being in the life to come. The best of our human experience found in history, philosophy, and the many religious traditions seems to be at times negated by both the development and/or presumptions of the newer disciplines of economics, biology, sociology and depth psychology.

How can we reconcile the positive elements and conclusions of these various disciplines with the basic concerns always present in the human condition? Because we are addressing the mystery of life and the mystery of God, we will always live with incomplete answers. We will find our way only when we continue to seek God as we seek true humanity, and we can only find truth about ourselves as we find truth about God.

Earlier we studied the nature of sanctifying grace and the scriptural foundation for our belief that we literally share in the divine life. Prior to that presentation, we found it necessary to reflect on the gift of free will, and then freedom and liberty as a result of free will properly used. Inasmuch as free will is native to our spiritual soul and we are made to the likeness of God, we have the capacity to love, and even to relate intimately with God Himself.

Since our basic theme in these concluding chapters is our relationship with God in faith, we need a clear understanding of our native capacity to acquire knowledge and the process involved. How can we know anything? How can we trust? How can we believe?

The science of epistemology addresses these questions and many others, but for our purpose a schematic analysis should be sufficient. (As an aside, the word "epistemology" comes from the Greek word pistis, which means "trust," and it examines the grounds on which one can say: "That statement of belief is trustworthy." A parallel in Hebrew is the word "amen.") You might hold, as many do, that our insight into, and our attainment of, knowledge comes primarily from reason. We certainly use our reasoning ability, but probably ninety percent of all knowledge comes from faith in others who are close to the evidence in a particular field of knowledge and are trustworthy. This is true both in personal relationships as well as in the pursuit of knowledge.

Knowing, loving and growing as persons requires risk, trust and an act of faith. Let me cite three quick examples of what I mean. An intimate loving relationship requires a risk and a trust: a risk because we become vulnerable; a trust because we place ourselves into the hands of another. In our learning process, the study of history depends on the observational skills of the persons who are the primary source and the ability and truthfulness of the writers down through the centuries. Our knowledge of science also depends on scholars engaged in primary research.

However, the first step in the learning process is consciousness of self. An infant (or, rather, a young child) becomes conscious of self when the realization comes that he or she is separate and distinct from everyone else. Knowledge outside of oneself begins by perception through the five senses. However, learning through the senses requires attention and often needs positive interest. For example, each day every person encounters through sight and hearing so much of which we have no interest. We do not make a judgment and do not retain much of the sense impressions that continually occur. Even when judgments are made, such as at an accident, an athletic event, or storm, one person's perception and memory will be different than another's.

The question before us now is: Why is it so important to

consider the sources and validity of knowledge? The answer is that we must consider the fundamental question of life that are basic to the purpose of our existence. Therefore, confidence in our learning process and in our sources of knowledge is imperative.

Our basic questions are:

First: Why was I conceived and born?

Second: Am I able to understand reality (i.e., the nature of the human person and the people and the world outside of myself)? Am I able to understand the nature of anything beyond the phenomena perceived by the senses? (People, places, activities, decisions and things.)

Third: What is the nature of my personal responsibility and my freedom to make the basic decisions that will affect my journey through life — i.e., do I have a free will? We have already considered free will, and later will consider personal responsibility in more depth.

You will remember from your early days of studying religion that the Baltimore Catechism stated that each and every one of us was created "to know, love and serve God in this world, and to be happy with Him in the next." I do not think that we have improved much on this answer, but since we are limited and think in categories, we need to have a deeper understanding of our capacity to know, our ability to make free choices, and the nature of love and grace.

Most of the various categories of knowledge that are ours are accepted on the word of another. Unless the matter concerns something that seriously affects our lives and our happiness, we rarely challenge the sources, and at times those sources (person or persons, books or newspapers) would reflect prejudice, or possibly the necessity to belong to a group, or protective indifference, or fear. Therefore, the different areas of information that come to us could have moved through one or another of these prisms. In that case, it is natural that a person would ask himself or herself these questions: Is the person sharing this information with me worthy of belief, and therefore credible? Is this person in a position to know what he or she is talking about? Is this person trying seriously to convey knowledge?

These three questions are a protective armor and protection for us, and often we accept one or the other sources not as definitive knowledge, but opinion. When the three criteria are met we have knowledge, by way of moral certitude. Moral certitude is certainly adequate for most of the areas of knowledge in life. Physical certitude has to do primarily with the evidence of the senses, rooted in the natural law. Yet, even in this approach to knowledge, our judgments are filtered through our past experiences, pleasant and unpleasant.

The only absolute certitude that we have is the fact of our existence and the consciousness of that existence, together with the principle of contradiction — i.e., that a thing cannot be and not be at the same time. Ultimately this principle is the basis for all our judgments. In the area of faith in revealed truths, we have a certitude of the existence of God and God's revelation, but that only comes to us through the gift of grace and faith that disposes us to accept these truths.

Unconsciously, many people equate the source of knowledge with reason, either inductive or deductive reason. As a matter of fact, reason is probably only the source of ten percent of our knowledge. Faith is the source of most of our knowledge, and reason is used to analyze the credibility of the sources.

Once we accept our consciousness (i.e., our intellectual awareness), we also spontaneously recognize the principle of contradiction and the essential trustworthiness of our ability to acquire knowledge. The act of knowledge seems a very simple thing. It is, however, a rather mysterious and profound experience.

In the routine of life, most of us accept what we know without too many questions. This acceptance encompasses intellectual knowledge as well as sense-knowledge. People gather facts in three basic ways:

Facts of everyday experience

1. Real world of substance; e.g., earth, sun and stars.

2. Space and space relations; e.g., here and there, outside and inside.

3. Time and time relations; e.g., yesterday, tomorrow, now, soon.

4. Mathematical and numerical quantities.

5. Qualities; e.g., blue, strong, intelligent, cold.

6. Actions, reactions, posture, habits.

Facts of sense experience

Each of us—or at least most of us—feels, hears, sees, tastes, smells, etc.

Facts of intellectual experience

Consciousness of the ego or "self," thoughts, knowledge, "soul," states of the will (such as "I must," "I ought not").

Every person is aware of the great distinction between self and things other than self; between mind and matter; between living and inanimate things; between subjective and objective; between ideal and real, etc. You will have noted that each of these categories, while they refer to specifics, are expressed in the abstract, and are universal concepts distinct from sense perception. Anything physical in the real world will be recognized through the medium of the senses. However, in the thought process, our experiences are classified by their nature and use. In technical language, we would call this "class-essence." These concepts are the result of a reasoning process both inductive and deductive. If they are accurate, universal ideas result and we can communicate.

Reasoning could be defined as the process by which the human intellect passes from what it already knows to what it does not yet know, without necessarily having recourse to new information. We continually use the reasoning process, but most of the data or information that we use in attaining new knowledge does not come from primary research or even immediate sources, but from books or theories or assumptions of others that we accept on faith. Therefore, while our reasoning process is very important, the validity of our conclusions depends on the credibility we place in someone else. Therefore, most of our knowledge rests on faith.

Faith of this nature is a pre-requirement for all scientific progress and cultural growth. If we wish to grow intellectually and further our knowledge, it is impossible to start from the beginning. We must accept and appreciate the treasure of experience and knowledge of those who came before us. We need to be directed by teachers whom we trust and whom we believe to be knowledgeable. Thus we ourselves are able to know, to understand, and to think and investigate further. One who wishes to learn must have faith. History, law and the sciences depend on witness and testimony, and cannot get along without faith.

Even though all intellectual disciplines depend on faith as a source of knowledge, faith is often misplaced and belief sometimes is naive. So we must ask ourselves the questions: What does faith mean? What is faith about? Is the word "faith" used differently in different contexts? In reality, these questions are both positive and negative. For example, if we say "I believe it will rain tomorrow," what we mean is "I have some reason to be sure, but I am not certain." In this context, belief is merely an opinion and conjecture. But the word "believe" can also express confidence, trust and fidelity. For example, if I say "I believe you," this is not some conjecture, but a deep certainty founded on personal trust. Consequently, belief is a word with many possible meanings; it may be misused and lead to confusion.

Reason and detachment must come into the thought process when we accept as certain knowledge shared with us by another and by a carefully researched subject. The principle of contradiction is fundamental to the reasoning process in accepting as true anything within the history of human knowledge. As we have previously stated, a thing cannot be and not be at the same time. In other words, the distinction yes and no, true and false, good and evil, cannot be given up unless we want to give up being human.

Faith simply stated means accepting something on another's testimony. Each person is unique and, in the search for knowledge and personal growth, must always make the distinction between opinion and certitude in his or her judgment. Let me share with you the natural mental process in making these judgments:

1. Opinion is a state of mind in which a person decides for the truth of a judgment, but with fear of the possibility of error. The best that the mind can attain with regard to truth of its judgment is a certain amount of probability. We often act on opinion.

2. Certitude is a state of mind in which a person gives a firm assent to a judgment without fear of error, due to recognized valid reasons.

3. Three elements enter into the concept of certitude:

a) the negative factor—the absence of fear of possible error;

b) the positive factor—consciously recognized valid reasons for the firm assent of the mind;

c) the understanding of valid reasons which exclude fear.

There are degrees of certitude: moral certitude, wherein motives of certitude based on the law of customary human conduct in a given environment under given conditions (for example, class schedules in a university); physical certitude, wherein certitude is based upon a physical law of nature and the latter is considered to be uniform, necessary, and universal (such as the law of gravity); and metaphysical certitude, which is based upon a metaphysical law, an exception to which is intrinsically impossible, because it would involve a contradiction in itself. The most basic expression of metaphysical certitude would be the acceptance of one's own existence.

Because we have the ability to make judgments with certitude in faith, we continue to have the treasure of experience and knowledge of those who came before us. Human interaction, human trust, human fidelity and love depend on such faith. As unique as every person is, he or she is open to others and finally open to the whole of reality. An anthropologist would say "open to the whole world." Because every person is responsible for his or her own life, everyone must work towards creating an environment for himself or herself in which he or she can move more freely in the order of time to his or her ultimate and eternal destiny. We know of our eternal destiny through divine revelation, which is the subject of our next chapter.

Chapter VIII

❧

Revelation
and
Evangelization

Alexander Pope once made a remark: "A little learning is a dangerous thing." This has been repeated often in succeeding generations—sometimes accepted as a serious truth, and at times repeated with a bit of sarcasm. If we limit our judgment to the criteria or modality of one particular discipline, the direction of our lives will be seriously limited. The sciences of physics, sociology, psychology, jurisprudence, political science, or anthropology cannot answer ultimate questions or offer the fundamental values of life.

We all know people who are knowledgeable in the arts and sciences, in business or in the professions, who have not seriously studied the truths of religion beyond junior high school. They are placing a tremendous burden on the "will" alone. We need to go back to the source of faith (i.e., God revealing Himself to us). For these reasons my subject now is the nature of revelation.

God speaks to us in the beauty and order of our planet earth and our solar system and in the vast scope of the Milky Way of which our solar system is but a minute part. God speaks to us in the mystery of human life and in the transcendental relationship of people to people. God speaks to us in the sharing of His word and the providential love with the Hebrew people from the time of Abraham to St. John the Baptist which concludes the Old Testament. God speaks to us, in this our order of time, in the birth, life, teaching, death, and resurrection of His Son, Our Lord Jesus Christ. The coming of Christ into the world is both the central point of human history and the center of salvation history. God speaks to us continually through the Holy Spirit, through His presence, gifts, guidance, and support.

When we reflect on the order and beauty of the universe, we should also approach this reflection with an awe similar to primitive humans, or even more so because of our sources of knowledge. Our knowledge, rooted in the heritage of history and research, in all fields is broader and deeper than was possible for people of earlier centuries. This knowledge has spawned an endless number of questions. Primitive humans stood in awe of the sun, moon, and the stars. We, in turn, because of the sciences of astronomy and astrophysics, are beginning to realize the extent of our ignorance of God's creation. For example, considering our own galactic system that we call the Milky Way, refined calculations bring us to the conclusion that the diameter of the Milky Way measures eighty thousand light years, and its thickness sixteen thousand light years. Our galaxy also contains one-hundred-thousand million stars. Our sun is only one of these millions of stars. You will remember that a light year is the distance that light travels in a vacuum for a period of one year (i.e., approximately 5.8 trillion miles). This illustrates what we mean by a natural mystery. The Hubble telescope has discovered another galaxy called "Virgo" that is fifty-two million light years from the earth.

We cannot visualize, and it is almost impossible for us to realize, the scope or size of the universe. In order to place this in a perspective with a measurement in miles, Pluto, within our own solar system, is two billion and seven hundred million (2,700,000,000!) miles from the earth. Light from the closest star traveling one-hundred-and-eighty-six thousand miles per second takes four years to reach the earth.

If we desire to think of a mystery closer to home, why not our nervous system with the thousands of cells controlling every function of our bodies? One illustration should be sufficient. Recently I read a paper of a neurologist that stated that one brain cell is capable of being connected with ten thousand other brain cells. Neurologists also tell us that there is an infinitesimal space between one cell and another, about a millionth of an inch, the cells being connected by electrical impulses.

God speaks to us in these complexities of nature. There is no possibility of these developments and relationships occurring by chance. In my early undergraduate days I became convinced of this, but only about twenty-five years ago did I hear a similar statement from one of the great scientists of our century. I was giving the baccalaureate sermon in a southern college and Dr. Werner von Braun was to give the graduation talk. (You will remember that he is the father of space travel.) Since we were both strangers in town, we went out for an evening meal together. During the course of the evening, he shared with me the history of his religious beliefs. He was from a good Lutheran family, and until his university experience shared the faith of his parents. In his preliminary research, he slipped into agnosticism. He told me that the more evidence he found in the order of the universe, he found it absolutely impossible to be an agnostic. At that time he was looking to bring together scientists and theologians to consider how religious insights can help better understand the ultimate questions of life. He died six months later. It was a sadness that he was unable to attain this goal.

As we address the basic questions of life, it seems natural for us to address them from a basis of what we know with an element of certitude. For that reason, when we think of revelation our starting point usually is with Abraham and Moses. Yet, salvation history did not begin with these two great patriarchs nor with recorded history. In God's creative love, salvation history would parallel intelligent life on this planet earth. If we speak of salvation history for primitive people, should we not also speak of revelation for them? One might say: "Now you are speculating." Historically, I would say "yes"; philosophically, "no." Since God created each person with the capacity of transcendence and the ultimate goal of transcendent relationship is God Himself, it is reasonable to conclude that God in some manner revealed Himself to people of all times.

The history of salvation (and therefore some form of revelation) would take place when each person in prehistoric centuries experienced freedom and was capable of directing his or her life, and also when communities interacted relative to rights, justice, human values and purpose of existence. God is always present, not only with His sustaining providence, but also with His grace. The grace of God is always at work with every person in human history. Just as we understand that the gift of faith is a grace that disposes us to accept revealed truth, so also grace to people of pre-recorded history would dispose them to know something of God and relate their lives to Him.

We always keep in mind that our knowledge of God in this order of time is always limited, and a mystery. In this life we will never fully understand God. In the history of Western thought, there have been two ways of affirming the existence of God. One argues from the notion of God that He must be; the other argues from the analysis of experience that He must be. The first is *a priori*; the second *a posteriori*. Judeo-Christian tradition concentrates on the second, but in human history the first approach seems always to have been present. This inherent approach is evident in the analysis of languages. We, and the people of any age, do not make language; we are born into it. In every language, we encounter the word "God." Language shapes the way we touch reality and allow it to touch us. It is the basis for communication, for reaching beyond ourselves into the lives of others. We exist united with others through language. It forms the questions we consider and the answers we give. Deep in language, part of its initial and primitive tradition, is the word "God."

While we do not know exactly how God communicated with pre-historic people, we do know of the longing for immortality and for God that is inherent in human consciousness that language evidences. The human mind always strives toward the understanding of reality, and discovers that the ultimate reality and cause of mortal and transient existence is a mystery that we call God.

Even though this a priori experience is present, it has always been limited; and persons, religions and cultures of every age have not been able to live up to the ideals inherent in gifts of human nature. The necessity of moral law is recognized, but the certitude of judgment and the capacity to live up to this law can be fulfilled only by supernatural revelation and grace. This can be demonstrated by the history of every nation and culture.

We read in St. Paul's letter to the Hebrews: "God Who spoke of old to the Hebrews through the prophets by many decrees and many ways has at last in these days spoken to us by His Son" (Hebrews 1:1 ff.). Christ often stressed the character of revelation in His teaching (Matthew 11:25-27; and Matthew 16, 17; and John 15:15). Again we read in St. John that this revelation which was given by Christ to the Apostles will be completed by the Holy Spirit (John 16:12 ff.). A theological understanding of revelation would be the history of the transcendental relationships between man and God which are constituted by God's self-communication. This communication is supernatural—i.e., grace given and made possible for every human mind to accept. In traditional religious teaching, it is called the gift of faith.

Each day in the Liturgy of the Word we read the first lesson from Sacred Scripture, and we say: "The Word of the

Lord." What do we mean when we sincerely make this statement? Certainly, God is not literally speaking to us, nor did
God dictate the various books of Sacred Scripture. Yet, in our
gift of faith we know that in the content of the books of the
Bible God is revealing to us eternal truths and His plan of salvation history.

The books of both the Old and New Testament are written in human language in different periods of history, reflecting different cultures, under the inspiration of the Holy
Spirit. In our Christian heritage, we rely on the Church instituted by Christ to authenticate the canon of the Bible.

Biblical studies and history tell us that the books of the
New Testament were written in the different early Christian
communities established by the apostles and evangelists, especially in communities established by St. Peter, St. John, St.
Matthew, and St. Paul. In other words, the books of the New
Testament were developed from the teaching of Christ and
the early traditions handed on by the apostles, fulfilling the
mandate of Christ to teach all nations.

In the development of theology in each century and generation, theologians and the Magisterium seek both through
Scripture and tradition to teach the message of God and the
human response to God's Word, in the order of time, always
looking forward to eternity. Both the interpretation of Sacred
Scripture and the development of theology must be approached with the realization of human limitation and the
mystery of God and the mystery of God's communication
with men and women of every century and generation.

The Old Testament provides the first approximations,
even though incomplete and provisional, of God's plan of
salvation. God's plan of salvation as presented in the Old
Testament was to be achieved in eschatology (i.e., the final
end of the human race). The sacred texts foreshadowed that
goal. The New Testament accepts this belief, but clearly states

that this final goal of mankind has been inaugurated and made present through Christ during His life on earth, which is the focal point of human history.

However, this goal will not be totally consummated until the people of every generation to the end of time have been called into existence by God and through death move to eternity. It is the mission of the Church to make its way toward that end. This Christian eschatology brings to our consciousness the consummation of all things, and challenges the people of the world to so live in preparation for that end.

Jesus recognized and accepted that He is at the center and climax of God's plan of salvation. Jesus' teaching and actions are present with us today as a consequence of His acceptance of God's plan. He preaches the good news of the kingdom (Matthew 4:17-23). He heals the sick and casts out evil spirits. In this manner, He shows that He is the One Who was to come (Matthew 11:3 ff.) and the kingdom of God is at hand (Matthew 12:28).

The earthly establishment of the kingdom will not take place by a sudden world transformation. The Word of God sown by Jesus will germinate slowly in hearts like the grain of seed in the earth. It will experience setbacks as well as brilliant successes (Matthew 13:1-9, 18-23). It will transform the earth like the leaven in dough (Matthew 13:22). In Sacred Scripture we learn that in God's plan of salvation a new period emerges between the fullness of time (the life of Jesus) and the end of ages (Matthew 28:10).

In the final analysis, our acceptance of supernatural revelation rests on our firm belief that Jesus is the Christ, the Son of God, the Messiah promised to the Jewish people. St. Paul, a Jewish scholar, graphically presented this analysis. He taught that the Jewish nation did not fully remain faithful to the covenant and they thought of the Messiah as a temporal leader. He stated clearly that certitude of faith, and therefore the acceptance of revelation, rests in a firm belief in the divinity of Christ.

But what does the divinity of Christ mean? We all can read the gospels and epistles. We see Christ as a man in His contact with other men and women from the moment of His conception until the moment of His ascension into heaven. In the gospels, we also see Him in His control over every phase of nature. We see Him manifested in His miracles, as well as the Sermon on the Mount. We see Him in the doctrine of charity—the personal commitment of love. We, as persons of every generation and century A.D., ask ourselves: Who is Christ? Here, the gift of faith, the disposition of the intellect by God, is essential. Christ is God, the Second Person of the Blessed Trinity, true God eternally existing. Christ is man possessing a human nature; living, walking, working, teaching, and dying for all. We, with the limitations of our human nature, in this life will never fully understand the mystery of the Incarnation—i.e., God the Son taking on our human nature and becoming one with us. We see Christ as the divine and human bridge between man and God, for Christ came into the world that each person might have union with God.

In responding to grace we begin slowly to realize what it means to have faith in Christ and in the truths He revealed. This faith is not something that can be halfhearted; it cannot be a lip service. This faith must be a positive commitment. We might say that faith is a personal realization, even more than an intellectual assent.

St. John tells us that: "He who does the truth comes to life." The will therefore is involved, and the word does as used by St. John is clearly descriptive of personal commitment. The doing of this truth brings about the union which is the commitment between myself and Christ. The recognition of this union, the knowledge that Christ dwells within my being, is the all-important insight of life.

To possess faith is to stake one's life on God's love. Until a person makes such a commitment, he or she does not possess faith. St. Luke records Christ's invitation: "If anyone would be my disciple, let him renounce himself, take up his cross and follow Me."

We who live in a world where everything is contingent and passing, in accepting revelation through faith in Christ move to an eternal reality that is absolute. Faith is an intellectual and volitional association wherein God takes and keeps the initiative. We are elevated from the natural to the supernatural, from our finite mind to the Infinite Mind. This union is of such a nature that it brings about a permanent relationship with God. Although the initiative comes from God, an enduring response is necessary from us.

Divine faith is correlative to revelation. Once a person possesses and lives the faith, his or her relationship with God is personal. It is a total decision of life and, in turn, offers to each person a security and a realization of his or her dignity. Living a life of faith and love is the essence of religion. A French theologian, Gabriel Marcel, stated this so well: "To put one's center of gravity in God and not in oneself. That is what is meant by religion."

It is a strange paradox of Christianity that we can only find ourselves by losing ourselves. Christ said: "No one goes to the Father except through Me." He is inviting us, leading us, as He says: "Come and follow Me."

It is the mission of the Church (therefore, your mission and mine) to help people to know Christ and in turn follow Him. This mission and vocation is called evangelization. In his encyclical, *Evangelii Nuntiandi*, Pope Paul VI wrote:

Evangelization is in fact the grace and vocation proper to the Church, her deepest identity. She exists in order to evangelize, that is to say in order to preach and

teach, to be the channel of the gift of grace, to reconcile sinners with God and to perpetuate Christ's sacrifice in the Mass, which is the memorial of His death
and glorious Resurrection.

Paul VI's notion of evangelization is more inclusive than that
of the kerygmatic theologians, who normally limit themselves to scriptural sources. In his view, proclamation and
catechesis, while occupying an important place in evangelization, are only one aspect of it. Evangelization, moreover,
should be directed not simply at individuals but also at cultures, which need to be regenerated by contact with the
Gospel.

The tasks of human development and liberation, according to the apostolic exhortation, are profoundly linked with
evangelization, but they are not the same thing. Against all
secularizing tendencies, Paul VI warned that evangelization
can never be reduced to a merely temporal project. It must always include a clear and unequivocal proclamation of Jesus
as Lord. It must be directed to eternal life in God.

Although the name of Jesus Christ must be explicitly proclaimed, evangelization can never be a matter of words
alone. "The witness of a Christian life is the first and irreplaceable form of mission" ("Redemptoris Mission"). Before
we can pass on the Gospel to others, it must first have permeated our own lives. As "Redemptoris Mission" said, "It is
important to recall that evangelization involves conversion,
that is interior change." It must emanate from a deep experience of God.

We limited human beings whose learning experience and
contact with each other begin with and depend on our five
senses have a difficulty of conceiving of a personal relationship with God because this love relationship completely
transcends the senses. Only in Jesus Christ Who in His divine

nature is the bridge that unites us with God can this super-natural union take place.

You will remember the prayer of Jesus a short time before He was arrested: "I do not pray for them alone. I pray also for those who will believe in Me through their word, that they all may be one as You Father, are in Me, and I in You; I pray that they may be [one] in us, that the world may believe that You sent Me...I living in them, You living in Me—that their unity may be complete. So shall the world know that You sent Me, and that You loved them as You loved Me." (John 17: 20-23). Knowing our limitations, mistakes, and sins, we wonder how God could love us as He loves His Son Jesus. In our next chapter, I will try to consider how in faith we can be open to God's word and love within these human limitations.

Chapter IX

Faith within Human Limitations

There is an old Italian proverb that says: "Whoever forsakes the old way for the new knows what he is losing, but not what he will find." We who have appreciated our gift of faith and know that it has been an anchor for us, both through successes and difficulties of life, have encountered people who have lost that anchor. Some have not nurtured their faith; some have slipped into a pragmatic approach to life; some have been dominated by a hedonistic pleasure lifestyle; and some have opted for a materialistic promise of power or security. Possibly they do not realize that they have surrendered to a distorted image of reality.

Because we hope to live in a real world that belongs to God, now we will consider how we live our faith within human limitations in our allotted time in this world. We must ask ourselves: Is our knowledge adequate? How do we relate to God, to our family, our associates, and to the natural laws in the world He created?

We begin to be open through faith in God's world when we acknowledge the mystery of ourselves. The basic question that each one of us asks is of the nature and source of our existence, which endures as the mystery of our lives from childhood to old age and death. It is the key question that is never completely answered, but is necessary to give meaning and quality to life.

The discipline that explores this question is a combination of philosophy and theology that is also a primary source for Christian anthropology, which considers the totality and origin of persons and cultures. Ultimate answers go beyond the biological, psychological and sociological conditions of humankind. We know that there is no single study, experience or relationship that can entirely explain us to ourselves. In asking the question, we have already transcended or gone beyond ourselves.

This constant questioning in human experience leads to the final question of our contingent existence and the source of all being, so we speak of God. I find no better way to consider "Faith Within Human Limitations" than to begin with the prologue of the Gospel of St. John, and St. Paul's Letter to the Ephesians (1:3-10). St. John and St. Paul poetically and graphically present the advent of the Son of God into the world of man in creation. In redemptive love, Christ is clearly recognized as the source of grace and truth throughout salvation history. He offers to each person an opportunity for eternal union with God as bonded in faith and love. Thus faith, as a gift, becomes an encounter with reality. As a virtue, it becomes a personal commitment to Christ and the truths He revealed to us.

An analytical study of faith could convey the impression of cold intellectual assent. This is far from true when faith is possessed; then faith produces a warm intellectual bond. This bond exists between God and each person, and this bond also holds together the members of the Christian community.

Faith cannot be static; it is not even static in any period of life. Faith is neither academic nor pedantic, but something living, constantly growing, and at times fragile. Faith, as a virtue, is, of course, a personal possession; for virtue, as well as knowledge and love, exists within the mind and will of each person as an orientation to life and security of being.

Faith is a gift of the Holy Spirit who enables us to give ourselves entirely to God and accept with confidence His eternal message. When we considered the validity of human knowledge in Chapter VII, we recognized that human faith is the primary source of knowledge that is monitored by reason. Divine faith is different in its source and orientation, even though the capacity to reason is the cognitive element of the supernatural gift of faith.

But if faith came only through analysis and synthesis (or even intuitive knowledge), it would then depend only on experiential data. Faith also is not dependent on feeling, no matter how profound. In the gift of faith, we are brought very truly and profoundly into contact with ultimate reality—i.e., with our origins and destiny with God Himself.

Our response to the gift of faith is a spiritual leap of confidence wherein when God reveals Himself to us, we respond. Knowledge gained through faith becomes an integral part of the personality and character of the possessor. He literally makes both the virtue and the knowledge his own. However, no one completely possesses anything upon a first encounter—whether knowledge, love or physical skills. This always requires a gradual process.

Experience illustrates this fact in daily activity. For the purpose of clarification, let us consider an example that is commonplace with all of us—that is, the growth or lack of growth of knowledge and the intimacy of human love.

During a course of casual or planned association, a young man and woman recognize the beginnings of interest in each other, and hope for a growth and development in personal relationship. Tentatively each begins to have an insight into the personality of the other, but despite initial understanding, they drift apart and cannot understand why. Other couples marry, and after some weeks are surprised and disturbed by their limited knowledge of each other. Some of these gradually begin to know each other better and their pristine love grows and develops. On the other hand, marriage counselors encounter couples who at the time or marriage were under the impression that they possessed mutual knowledge and interests, and whose marriages fail upon dis-covery that such was not the case. They became inarticulate, and through a lack of communication drifted apart.

The sad fact exists that some husbands and wives who have lived with each other twenty years cannot engage in conversation. Any human communion or relationship grows and develops in the manner in which the persons involved know and accept the personality and qualities of others.

A relationship between God and man, while similar, does not completely parallel this pattern or growth or retrogres-sion. God Who is eternal, infinite in all perfections, does not change; His gifts are constant. God clearly reveals truths con-cerning Himself and the human race. Providentially, He sus-tains human existence, and shares His divine life of love. Initially a person may accept both the gifts of knowledge and love but later, in times of stress and temptation, may follow the line of the least resistance; then, through concentration on self, ignores the divine gifts and becomes absorbed by the things of the world—i.e., money, power, pleasure or person-al success. Such a person has introduced disorder into life; and while the disorder exists, faith cannot grow.

Faith is never exclusive; it is both received within the faith community and shared with others. God called us into being (i.e., into existence) and works with us according to the na-ture that He gave us. Since our nature is social, revealed truths come to us through normal human contacts. A survey of our own experience will afford some insight. Most of us in our professional work, home, and civic responsibilities have a measure of success, but even in the obtaining of our objec-tives a vacuum seems to exist and our efforts strike us as fu-tile. These efforts are limited to specific objectives of the here and now. Yet, on occasion we encounter a person whose character is above the norm, a person who is truly poor in spirit and almost completely detached from the things of the world. We ask ourselves the reason for this detachment, and we seek to understand the motives of this person's unselfishness.

Another acquaintance may consistently evidence an objective approach in conversation and make correct and truthful judgments and generous commitments even though the outcome would be contrary to his or her own desires. This person would seem to be operating against his or her own best interests, and we ask ourselves why. What is the source of this courage and unselfishness? It is the gift of faith which enables a person to rise above the limited good of this world, and rarely is such detachment achieved without it.

I can recall individuals who have been open to receive the gift of faith principally because the lives of friends and acquaintances forced them to think. A priest friend belongs in this category. His introduction into my friendship was abrupt.

As a political science student at the university where I was teaching, he came into my office unannounced. Apparently frustrated, he began, with no preliminaries: "I've got a crazy roommate!" He had an air of discovery mingled with his frustration, and it was difficult to break through his intensity for introductions. "Why do you make such a statement?" I inquired. "My roommate gets up at six o'clock every morning and comes over to this chapel. He is not putting on an act, of that I am convinced. At the beginning of the semester I said he would cut this out fast, but I was wrong," he continued.

This young visitor had an excellent mind, and from this initial contact pursued religious instructions all summer. He was ordained a priest a few years later. The beginning of his faith was the example of the roommate who rose early every morning to pray, attend Mass, and receive Communion. For the first time in his life he saw a personal commitment motivated by the love of God. Since he was a student in the true sense of the word, he was forced to ask the basic question: Why?

All Christians approach faith in their early years with simplicity; their lives are not complicated; they are confident. Christ said: "Whosoever shall not receive the kingdom of God as a little child, shall not enter into it." He did not mean that one should be childish intellectually, but completely honest and open as a child.

It is sad but true that even adults confuse simplicity with childishness. A child's approach to religion is similar to the acceptance of his mother's "do's" and "don'ts" accepting all of her dictums. A child is not capable of approaching faith in any deeper manner. But faith is of the intellect, and the intellect is disposed to recognize truth. The individual of necessity must work to acquire knowledge. Everyone needs to apply the mind to truth. How can anyone of mature years who has never applied his or her mind to the study of religious truths possibly have anything more than a childish faith? It is impossible, because such a person is intellectually a child as far as an approach to faith is concerned.

I know people, college graduates, who have never opened a book on religion after leaving junior high school. This is a strange and dangerous situation. Faith is an intellectual virtue for the possession of which everyone must use their intellect. An adult who never reads places a tremendous strain on intellectual powers. Such a person encounters questions which come into conflict with a tenet of faith armed with the only answer he or she is capable of giving: that the Church says so. Surely that is not an adequate answer to any question for a person capable of learning.

Every rational being is capable of understanding the truths of human nature which Almighty God has revealed. One who does not study places all of the effort of decisions on the will, whereas faith is first of the intellect and only then of the will. So a person of necessity must become informed, and must go beyond the precepts of the Church in personal growth.

Following the laws of the Church does not necessarily mean that one grows in faith. The laws are only guidelines and helps. We mature spiritually only when we encounter and accept truth revealed by God, and we cannot accomplish this in any other manner. Faith must grow with the intellectual insight of the truths revealed.

Each one of us is unique and cannot depend on another for growth in faith. The grace of God is present in all periods and in all circumstances of our lives, and each of us responds in a personal manner. Because of free will, even spiritually we are not exactly the same as any other person. The world belongs to God, and all things must be used in relation to His providence. We can be spiritual adults only if we grow to the maturity that stems from faith and love.

What is an adult? In my judgment, an adult is one who recognizes objectives and principles of life, possesses integrity and also has the courage to live up to that which he or she believes. An adult is one who can forget personal desires and reach out and take care of others.

Surely we should be adults in religion. We are not going to be adults in religion if we limit ourselves to merely accepting the gift of faith. Growth in religion is not only a matter of knowledge, but also a matter of courage and love. This adult commitment is a daily process, not an isolated volitional act. Certainly it is not satisfied only by attending Mass on Sundays and fulfilling our family responsibilities. These are manifestations. A religious adult is a person who understands that this is a world that comes from the creative love of God in which all things are ordered to God and have meaning only as they are directed to Him.

Certainly, in God's providence we hope to be religious adults; and if we are, happiness results. Happiness stems from the possession of essential good—that is, happiness comes from the attainment of the objective of the will which always must seek that which is good. We might have deviations because of weaknesses that are ours. We might experience sadness because of loss of a particular good, or pain from physical disorder, or disillusionment from too much confidence in another human being; but if we are personally committed to God, our lives are never disordered, only disrupted; and we have true happiness.

While faith is a personal gift and happiness a personal possession, we still recognize that Christ works through the society that He instituted. This continues in His Church of the twentieth century. Throughout life, we have heard Christ through the Gospels: "As the Father has sent Me, I also send you." "He that hears you hears Me, he who despises you despises Me." The vitality of faith must be recognized in society.

May I suggest the reading of one of the gospels in one sitting for a cohesive insight to the vitality expected in the followers of Christ. Christ did not come to save the people of Israel alone, nor to teach a few people in a rather small territory. He came to reconcile the human race with His heavenly Father and He came to redeem the human race. This redemption is eternal because Christ is God. Christ came into the world in the order of time, but during the first century through the medium of His human nature He taught and influenced very few people. The effect of His teaching was to be recognized in future centuries within the social content of each generation.

The redemption through Christ is received by each of us in the particular generation in which we are born. For us, it is the twentieth century. We are learning today, and our approach to the doctrine of Christ is conditioned and colored by our background, our interests, our prejudices. We are learning from other men and women. We recognize that Christ looked forward to this condition; that through the efforts of other persons the truths that He taught would be offered down through the years.

One might suggest, with some exaggeration, that the reason why the world is not Catholic today rests primarily with Catholics. I would like to think that all we would need to do is live a Christian life, and in so living we would reflect the teaching and love of Christ and thus enable others to have an understanding of the dignity inherent in human nature and an insight into the purpose of human existence. Then no one could rationally deny the truth of the living presence of God.

Unfortunately this concept is too simplistic because of evil, free will, and the desire to maintain the "status quo." Yet Christ also came into the world to enable His followers to teach, and He is teaching through men and women—i.e., the human element of the Church. Since a notable percentage among us does not live entirely according to our stated principles, it is not surprising that some questions exist in the minds of persons who do not possess the gift of faith. Observers cannot separate the Church from its members. If the members in a given society do not reflect the social and supernatural doctrine of Christ, obviously the effectiveness of these doctrines will not be realized in that community.

History continually reflects human limitations within the Church. In some centuries the deviations have been very serious; in others much less so. However, the providence of God precludes the possibility of a loss of the content of faith, and His promise guarantees that eternal truths will be presented to men and women until the end of time (see St. Matthew's last chapter).

Despite human weakness, the Church grows. We recognize this in the religious history of succeeding generations. The decisions of the Councils down through the years mark a radical change in the presentation of doctrine and the accepted order in discipline and policy. Christ has commissioned us (the living Church of every century) to speak to people in the circumstances of their lives, penetrating their thought patterns, and by example demonstrating the happiness and stability of a community bonded by divine love.

I would like to conclude this presentation on faith within human limitations by sharing an analysis of the theological reflections of Father Karl Rahner:

> The most radical presupposition of [knowledge and] worship is that we finite creatures are able to enter into a relationship with the infinite creator. The unceasing wonder of worship is that it is a dialogical relationship with the absolute mystery; an event in which we are graciously addressed by God and, in turn, gratefully respond to Him. Any basic defense of the idea of worship must establish our openness to this dialogue with God.

This is an acknowledgment that our very being comes from and rests in God. Rahner claims that just such a fundamental openness to God is the essence of what it means to be human. A transcendental orientation toward the absolute mystery of God is what makes it possible for us to engage in the essentially human activities of knowing and choosing. Our ability to know or choose anything depends upon our ability to transcend everything in a movement which reaches toward the infinite horizon of the mystery of God. Why is this the case?

In order to know anything as one thing and not something else, we must transcend it and grasp it against a horizon of other possibilities. We always comprehend the specific objects of our knowledge against some such horizon. Ultimately, we grasp these particular horizons against an unlimited horizon which is beyond the realm of everything finite. Everything that we know in this world has a beginning and end. We always must contrast the contingent with the ultimate source. This ultimate horizon cannot be an object of the same kind as the ones whose knowledge it makes possible. For then it, too, would be an object within our world and would require a horizon against which it could be known. It must be that which has no horizon; that which cannot be transcended. And since it is by transcending the objects of our knowledge that we are able to define and comprehend them, this infinite horizon which cannot be transcended must be that which always remains indefinable and incomprehensible. This horizon must be the absolute mystery of God.

But that is not to say that God cannot be known. For Rahner, absolute mystery is not that which cannot be know, but rather that which cannot be mastered. We can and do know God; we just can never know God completely. In fact, we implicitly know the unfathomable mystery of God, the unlimited horizon which makes all our knowledge possible, whenever we know anything.

We do know ourselves in our natural and limited ability to communicate with our contemporaries. Those who have died have left us a share of their knowledge and love. We hope that when we leave this life we in turn will leave a legacy for those who follow after us. That hope is well founded because truth and love are not limited to the order of time. We will understand this in greater depth as we reflect on our unity with Jesus Christ, which we consider in the next chapter.

Chapter X

Christ and the
Human Ability
to Accept Faith

Albert Einstein (who probably has influenced the field of physics more than any other person in recent centuries) had an insight into the necessity of gratitude comparable to his genius. May I share with you his insight, and I quote:

> A hundred times every day I remind myself that my inner and outer life are based on the labors of other men, living and dead, and that I must exert myself in order to give in the same measure as I have received and am still receiving.

The same can be said of each of us (we have received from so many), but this truth pales in the face of the reality of our gift of existence—i.e., our very being—made to the image and likeness of God Himself. In the nature of our soul, our spiritual being, destined for eternal life, we recognize God's love as going even beyond our gift of existence to the sharing in the redemptive love of Christ. In the light of these gifts, we must consider our subject at hand: Christ the center of faith and human ability to accept faith. As you begin this chapter, please read the Epistle of St. Paul to the Colossians (1 & 2:12-20).

We who live towards the end of the twentieth century join Christians of two thousand years in making an extraordinary claim. We believe without hesitation that Jesus Christ is the key and center of all history. We claim that the life, teaching, and person of Jesus shed light on every dimension of human experience. He is the final and full revelation of God in human history. As we read in St. John: "He has the words of eternal life" (John 6:68). This is our central faith claim. How can we make this claim credible to others?

Because of human limitations and different cultural backgrounds, individual views will vary; but the belief common to all Christians is that in and through a faith relationship to Jesus each person can find God and therefore salvation. This relationship is personal to each of us in encountering the life, teaching, death, resurrection, and redemptive love of Jesus. We enter into the mystery of God's own self and are offered divine forgiveness and life.

Biblical scholars, theologians, and historians down through the centuries have tried to understand the mystery of the union of the creator with those whom He created with some limited success. However, both for the scholars and ourselves, insight and appreciation of this relationship is realized and internalized only in prayer.

Having recognized and accepted our human limitation and the mystery of God, we still need to grow in an understanding of truths revealed. The motive of faith rests in God Who revealed Himself to us, and also revealed essential truths concerning the meaning and purpose of life. The virtue of faith is the obedience and ordering of the intellect to God. It is the acceptance of a gift from God wherein the intellect is disposed by grace to accept truths revealed.

God has taken the initiative, and we respond to His invitation. Remember from Sacred Scripture His call: "Come, follow Me." Our response is not only an intellectual insight, but an acceptance of love. When love is sufficiently strong to enable us to become detached from intellectual pride, we yield ourselves to the testimony of God and faith becomes complete. The testimony of God comes to us through the person of Jesus Christ, and whoever accepts the divinity of Christ potentially embraces the whole of revelation.

The acceptance of the truths of revelation is not academic in character, but is a fulfillment of one's being in the quest for happiness. We have already recognized that happiness is a personal state of being that results from the possession of that which is in harmony with nature and grace. Faith as an insight into reality is not achieved except through grace, and is not complete without fulfillment in love. Only love can enable a person to rise above prejudice and comfort in unfounded assumptions.

A research chemist works long hours in a laboratory searching for truth, for an understanding of relationships of elements that are detached from personal fulfillment. A music lover enjoys the power and beauty of a full symphony orchestra, but enjoys expression, not possession. But one who seeks to know God, who seeks the fulfillment of his being, must possess, enjoy and love that which he seeks.

Love is a need basic to human nature and is enkindled only by the recognition and possession of the goodness of the one loved. St. Thomas in his analysis of faith states that the faith that unites us to God is due to its supernatural power of penetrating through the formulas of revelation to the reality beyond them.

Even in this life, a person begins a penetration beyond phenomena and time. On this earth, a person begins to share the life of God and begins to possess the power to transcend the temporal, to rise from the natural to the supernatural, to move from the limited approach of analogical knowledge to the direct approach of infused insight. Grace is the source of this power   St. Thomas Aquinas again tells us that "to believe is to give under the empire of the will, moved by grace, the assent and adherence of our intelligence to the Divine Truth." I can believe in the existence of God through reason, but I can know God only through the gifts of grace and faith.

The natural potential of the intellect does not attain ultimate truth. While a person thinks in the abstractions of universal ideas, all abstractions are limited by the particular judgments of experience, association, and research. Any knowledge of God acquired through experience and reason must also be analogical in character. God so known through His creation cannot be known as He exists in Himself. Surely it is reasonable to believe in the existence of God through knowledge of His creation, but it is not possible to know and understand the nature of God through an analogy of His creatures.

The study of human personality necessarily requires an analysis of the intellect and the will. The nature of the thought process demands a theoretical separation of these spiritual powers. Obviously, the separation is only analogical, not actual, for they are operative faculties interrelated in the action of each person who is separate and unique—different from all others.

In this process we begin to know a person and we are attracted or repelled by his or her actions, judgments, and decisions. We may conclude that this person possesses integrity and we love him or her, or possibly we recognize that he or she lacks this most essential element of character and we reject a close personal relationship.

In a similar manner, grace and charity are never isolated from faith. It is the intellect that recognizes truth that leads to belief, but the will is not absent from believing; in the gift of faith, our intelligence is disposed to admit the testimony of God, our of love for Him and the truths He reveals. The very essence of faith requires love, and it is love that enables a person, having recognized truth, to yield entirely in commitment and conduct.

The love that enables each person to accept complete intellectual assent of faith is a vital combination of the divine and human spiritual life. God offers a higher life without destroying the natural life. Through sanctifying grace and faith, God wills to communicate His own life and knowledge to us.

Christ said: "I am the way, the truth and the life." When we possess faith, we totally embrace this statement. We are no longer groping for an answer to the meaning of existence. We do not possess a truth, but the truth; not a life, but the life. The revelation of Christ possesses an internal consistency. The principles never change; the doctrine absorbs and orients all discoveries and cultures of succeeding centuries. Revelation and creation must exist in harmony, for their source and sustaining power is the same—God. Therefore, revelation and the truths of science can never be in conflict. If there is an apparent conflict, either a mistake has been made about a revealed truth or in a conclusion of a scientific study.

The possession of any particular human good and the seeking of any particular limited objective are not necessary in themselves for happiness. An alternative good or objective is always available. Thus cultures and discoveries are modified, lost, absorbed, without serious difficulty. Faith, on the contrary, has an absolute and final quality. This absolute assent seems impossible to a person who has directed his or her life on the basis of probabilities. Such total commitment seems impossible to the person who does not know of the power and goodness of God; who does not realize that both the motives and the means of faith must be supernatural. We must recognize the difference between the gift of faith and our understanding of the truths revealed by God.

The truths of faith come in two ways; externally to everyone through history and revelation; and internally to those who accept the supernatural gift and possess the supernatural virtue. Faith, considered as a vital force in life, must be internal. Revelation of the supernatural life is the revelation of the love of God, while revelation and love possessed is personal. In the Old Testament, the prophet Jeremiah anticipated this gift of faith and love: "With unchanging love I love thee, and now in mercy I have drawn thee to Myself."

A difficulty exists and will continue to exist if we approach faith and love solely on a theoretical level. Possessed of these supernatural gifts of God, we are not limited to a theoretical approach, but realize and enjoy them in the vitality of life's decisions. In the spiritual sphere of life, the supernatural virtues enable us to take a decisive position in all activities of life by placing the love of God at the center of human life. Fraternal charity follows from the love of God, and the corporal and spiritual works of mercy include all people, not merely those to whom we are attracted.

How else could one begin to understand and accomplish the two-fold command of Christ: "Love your enemies; do good to them that hate you; and pray for them that persecute you and calumniate you"; "Thou shalt love the Lord thy God with thy whole heart, and with thy whole soul, and with thy whole mind...Thou shalt love thy neighbor as thyself."

Through the insight of the gift of faith and the strength of love, we can judge ourselves and our neighbor in relationship to God and love God in ourselves and our neighbor. Otherwise, we are stifled not only by our faults, but also by our limited qualities and virtues. If I love myself as a creature, I am an egoist. If I love myself because I consider myself intelligent and I want others to appreciate my good qualities, I am just conceited. When God commands the love for neighbor as for self, He refers to the true character and source of love. He demands that we recognize the presence of the love of God within our own souls, that God is both the source and the ultimate goal of our existence.

Thus, with the strength of love and the stability of knowledge, we approach our neighbor who is destined for union with God either actually or potentially. The power and orientation of this supernatural love produces a detachment from self, from human respect, and from an exaggerated desire for personal recognition. The resulting objectivity produces a true insight into the reality of existence and an appreciation of the inherent dignity of a person in relationship with God.

The Sermon on the Mount truthfully might be called the charter of Christian life. The beatitudes are unintelligible if considered only in human relationship. However, if the beatitudes are accepted as a true orientation of man to God, they bring to their possessor a happiness that cannot be measured. The intellect and will work together. No one can believe and make such a total commitment of his or her life unless he or she wills to do so. There is always a fear of losing control.

St. Augustine long ago clearly explained that fear, common to all of us, is overcome only by the submission of one's will to God. The same spiritual gift that attracts a person to faith warns that its acceptance demands a transformation of life. Each person will need to change his or her whole outlook on life, and thus will need to live according to the beatitudes.

The difficulty is not intellectual in character, but in the necessity of interior change rooted in choice. Personal honesty and integrity are necessary to recognize and accept moral responsibility. When a person wants to do something seriously morally wrong, or deny a truth of faith, he or she must do violence to the intellect through a rationalization process in order to live at peace (e.g., in an abortion, calling the action a freedom of choice rather than addressing the real issue of taking the life of an unborn child).

Faith sets up a new relationship between God and those who were formerly guided by experience alone. God, truly the father, instructs His children in language they can understand. He has accomplished this directly and immediately in the person of God the Son as He lived in the world with us in the person of Jesus the Christ.

In faith one realizes that the truths taught by Christ are

absolute and unchangeable, for their source is God Himself. The content of faith is the knowledge of the Divine Person, Christ, and the truths He reveals. This insight into the goodness of God is also recognized as the source of love. The security of knowledge, combined with the force of love, provides the vitality that lifts the Christian above the limitations of the life span of human knowledge and attainments.

In the chapter concerned with the relationship of the natural and the supernatural, an attempt was made to delineate this source of Christian vitality. God, when He adopts us as His children, transforms us into new beings totally beyond the legal effect of human adoption. When God adopts us into His family, we literally have a share in the divine life. God, through love, is the source of our being in creation and in grace becoming children of God. When we share divine life, it is also possible for us to share divine knowledge. St. Paul tells us that a Christian does not only think with his own intellect, but through faith he has the use of the mind of Christ.

The intellectual independence or mental autonomy so prized by all of us is not possible because of insufficient insight into being—i.e., because of an inadequate grasp of reality. Freedom is of the will and is always limited because of insufficient evidence to make certain judgments of ultimate truths. Once the mind has an insight as to the truthfulness of a judgment, it is not free to reject the truth. Because of the insufficiency of evidence, even in critical matters, a person often must judge and act on the basis of opinion. Divine faith that is informed eliminates this intellectual uncertainty in matters of revealed truth and morality. And, it enables one for the most part to form clear and certain judgments because the evidence is of divine origin.

This faith is a personal encounter with God, and through a free and unreserved acceptance brings about an intellectual security and deep peace. The soul of man, with a native ability to comprehend and love, takes a radical and definite turn toward its destiny and happiness. God is the ultimate reality, the supreme good; and in revelation and grace, He offers Himself to every person, in the eternal presence of Jesus Christ (Hebrews 7:24-27).

Each of us in the order of time begins the pursuit of knowledge and happiness that will be complete only in eternity through knowing and possessing God in the beatific vision. Even in this life, the knowledge and insight attained will satisfy the desire for certitude; for one with the gift of faith has positive, even though limited, knowledge. This knowledge acquired is the first step to a full and direct intellectual union with God in eternity.

Such an objective necessarily is accompanied by humility and simplicity which cuts through the complexity and disorder of the many secular goals. A person then moves in society with confidence, is unafraid, is eager to learn, and hopes that others will possess this certain criterion of truth—i.e., faith and the security of love. Love and faith are never separate, but are integral to the vital life of a person united with God. We are a People of God capable of thinking, willing, and acting in faith, hope, and charity.

While we are a people of God, we live in a world where many ignore God's laws and even live as if God did not exist. In the following chapter, hopefully this subjective morality can be addressed in some depth.

Chapter XI

❦

Subjective Morality Versus Revealed Truth

In our society we tend to place people in categories, recognizing them for their mastery in a given field, and sometimes looking for their opinions or judgments in areas where they have no expertise. For example, athletes and movie stars are used in advertising and public policy positions, sometimes to the detriment to morality or the common good. We have all kinds of titles for people who are the focal point of influence and service. We have master builders, master painters, ringmasters, toastmasters, school masters; we have maestros and mayors; so many are seeking master's degrees.

But in life there is something much more important: Do we have a mastery of ourselves? Are we in charge of our lives? This chapter addresses subjective morality as contrasted with revealed truths and natural law.

For fourteen years, the space and time of my life and energy was focused on the campus of a secular university. I worked as campus minister and taught philosophy and theology. The intellectual and social life of a university community was almost a microcosm of life in these United States.

Moral problems and intellectual confusion were more marked at the university than those of the general public because of the immaturity of students and the philosophies and ideologies of some faculty members. Both from experience in teaching and in counseling, I came to the conclusion that most people who had a difficulty in accepting objective norms of morality did so for one of three reasons: because of a lack of understanding of these norms; or from unfounded assumptions; or from a purely subjective approach to moral values. Since the basis of their judgments so often did not correspond to reality, on those occasions they did not live intellectually and emotionally in a real world, but in a world of fantasy. Tunnel vision, or a lifestyle dominated by personal desires and unfulfilled needs, resulted.

People who do not accept revealed truths, or who ignore revealed truths and objective norms of justice in making judgments in business or the professions, so often consider the size of a bank account as more important than the right of an employee to a living wage. Economic greed, emotional bias and fear of social pressure occasion disorders in justice and charity within the areas of race relations, economic systems and political policies. Many people on every level of the economic ladder and social scale have substituted phrases for logic, emotion for love, and the status quo for constructive planning.

A similar disorder occurs in interpersonal relationships when personal satisfaction, ambition, or the seeking of pleasure supersede the rights of others. The following examples should illustrate these disorders or disvalues. On one hand, we hear the use of the term freedom of choice rather than that of abortion which more clearly speaks of the taking of human life. In other instances, we often hear teenagers get into difficulty when they confuse spontaneous sex attraction with love. Or, at times people of all ages, because of their desire for acceptance or approval, will give in to pressure from their peers against their better judgment in moral matters or policy. Since we are concerned about the stability, integrity and happiness of people who are making judgments that affect their lives every day, the question that comes to us is: How general are these conditions?

More than fifty percent of the people of the United States are not regular in the practice of religion. In England and France the percentage is closer to eighty. The very few who try to arrive at a value system on a theoretical level are able through their efforts to become good humanists. We know from history that only a small percentage succeed. The end result is, for so many others, a lifestyle either dominated by a laissez-faire attitude, or at best they slip into the hope for personal security and satisfaction in this world.

Catholics and other Christians, Jews and Muslims are not immune from these tendencies. Many, consciously or unconsciously, try to separate business, professional, or political life from personal moral convictions and religious life. Let me share with you one example of situations that confront people in the business and professional world. Several years ago, an architect came to see me concerning a decision his firm must face. The firm was offered a contract to design a bridge over the Mississippi River. The cost would be in the millions of dollars. The awarding of the contract was contingent on adding five percent in excess of the actual bid. The five percent would go to the people awarding the contract. The question was since the bribery will take place regardless of who gets the contract could the architect be justified in accepting the condition? He refused and lost the contract.

Those who try to separate moral convictions from professional or political life try to restrict the social and moral teaching of their churches to a theoretical consideration of moral principles. Because of this dichotomy, they make judgments in the practical order solely in relationship to immediate goals and objectives. They unconsciously fall into a pragmatic approach to decision-making in moral judgments.

A surprising percentage of sincere and active members of churches or synagogues possesses only a vague and fragmentary notion of social justice and think that personal judgment on morality supersedes the common good. Let me cite an example. Often these active church goers do not recognize that systemic injustice results from economic or governmental policies that ignore the rights of workers or the common good. Personal sin or malice may not be present but decisions ignoring the common good still cause suffering and the loss of basic securities in life.

The absence or loss of religious commitment inevitably brings about a loss of love. Justice will not long prevail without love. The best of human philosophies and natural religions ultimately recognize this and concentrate on the dignity and perfection of the human person. For example, the idealism of Plato or the personal values of a modern humanist offer hope, but without the means of overcoming selfishness and control of the passions. History has demonstrated that good natural qualities will in individual cases enable some persons to grow in charity and justice. For society as a whole, however, justice and charity have not been the universal norms.

All we need to do to verify this is to look at the worldwide social experience in the twentieth century. The political and social philosophies and policies of the communist countries, ultimately brought about an internal collapse of the social and economic structures. The superman Nordic white supremacy ideology of the Nazis brought about untold human suffering and a World War. Public education systems throughout the United States has created an intellectual and moral vacuum in the lives of young people thus denying them the knowledge essential for personal growth and stability and security in society. One only need to read the daily newspaper to recognize so many other conditions that exist to the detriment of society in the absence of religious values.

Yet, for a believing Christian who accepts revelation, justice and charity are not only possible, but become an integral part of life. Happiness results; it is not limited to this world, but begins in time with the potential of perfect happiness beyond death. The dignity of each person comes from a personal relationship with God.

The reality of God and the true nature of every human being become clear in the person of Christ. Christ is an historical person and can be recognized as present in the first century as we measure time and not confused with religious myths. In Christ the love of God becomes recognizable, available and active. Only when a person submits to — and unites himself with — the love of God, does he see the ultimate meaning of life and the possibility of attaining its purpose.

Difficulties will always be present, but grace, the redemptive love of Christ shared, is also always present. St. Thomas Aquinas in the framework of Aristotelian logic explains the basic concept of grace by stating in essence: "God moves the will of man without offering violence to its freedom. The grace of God is antecedent to decision and enables the intellect to recognize the gulf between God and man while prompting the will to move towards fulfillment."

Each person responds to grace and revelation freely, and because of this people live on different levels of virtue and depth as realized in personal commitment. Yet we encounter some Catholics in our day who consider grace and divine providence like the ancient Semi-Pelagians—i.e., their concept of a virtuous life is the development of natural abilities with some assistance from Almighty God. They would hold that as long as people try to live a good life, God will assist them when they are confronted by temptation or weakness. Others recognizing personal guilt and the need for forgiveness, equates grace with the need for forgiveness and the remission of punishment. They approach God on a contractual basis, almost a *quid pro quo*—i.e., "I'll do this if you'll do that." In complete contrast to this mechanistic approach, there are people who confuse feeling and emotional experience with divine intervention and grace.

The agnostic, the humanist, the fundamentalist, and the

Catholic who primarily depends on structure have something in common: They all have a confused concept of a person's spiritual potential in relation to divine intervention. Their explanations, however, differ radically. Those who accept some form of predestination conclude that human nature is totally depraved, that man does not possess a potential for living a good life, but that fallen nature can be covered up and hidden by the redemption of Christ.

Another form of predestination holds that human nature is just inadequate, but some people are eternally called by God to salvation. Those who exaggerate the potential of human nature confuse natural kindness and justice with holiness. All they hope for seems to be that a person be kind to old people, generous to the poor, courteous to ladies, truthful to gentlemen and socially acceptable.

This has only an indirect relationship with holiness. Holiness is a nearness to God. People cannot be holy in the absence of love from God and for God. They can be naturally good, or naturally kind, but cannot be naturally holy. One is naturally kind if a friend is sick and in trouble and one lends assistance or a compassionate ear. Christ said that even pagans can be kind to friends. Christ was radical. He said: "Love your enemies, be good to them that hate you, pray for them that persecute you."

We as followers of Christ must also be radical. While living in the world, we must acknowledge and accept the sovereignty of Christ. We must have the courage of decision; we must recognize that a personal moral order is possible only when as rational beings we return to the source of our existence. If so, we will not be unbalanced by the trials, troubles, and vicissitudes encountered in life, but will accept these difficulties as transient experiences that cannot disorder the essential nature of one's being or the potential for happiness. Through grace, one shares in the certitude of divine providence and the freedom of divine love.

The happiness that follows the acceptance of the sovereignty of God parallels the intellectual security that accompanies knowledge through faith. God in the person of Jesus took humankind's destiny upon Himself. One who accepts the fact that God the Son became man also accepts the divine evaluation of human nature. God the Son, Who called us into being, entered into relationship with us in such a manner that in His human nature He could represent us in redemption and, at the same time, permit us to remain free.

God is not constrained by the need for control that a human exercises when he offers a gift, or the need for reciprocity in human love. Just as He created each person with the capacity to act freely, so also He offers His divine love to every man or woman with the same capacity for freedom. Yet the power of God's love is so strong and the potency for happiness is so great that a person can reject God only through malicious pride.

Personal dignity and freedom enable each of us to determine our own actions, possess a true knowledge of ourselves, and fulfill the objectives of our nature. We are not tools to be used, animals to be played with, or pieces of property available for disposal. Each person is unique and irreplaceable. Each person possesses a personality and worth independent of others. No one can be eliminated from existence and no person would exchange his or her own unique autonomy with any other person.

God in His creative love granted to each of us this dignity. God the Son in His redemptive love restored to us the potential for fulfillment of our being and happiness that was lost through sin. Although each of us possesses the dignity of freely directing our life, we recognize that freedom is within the created order of limited goods and objectives, and that no person is completely self-sufficient. Each of us has the capacity to transcend ourselves and give ourselves to others before we can attain the fulfillment of our personality.

Sacred Scripture often records the strong paradox that "man must lose himself before he can find himself." The kind of loss described here refers to loss of the pride of independent autonomy. Sacrifice and detachment will protect us against the stultifying experience of being locked within the limitations of our personal strengths and weaknesses. The transcendental character that releases us from ourselves must go even beyond human relationships and communion for the attainment of the happiness and potential intended by God. The goodness and beauty that we find in others, although wonderful and enabling us to grow, is inadequate and comes to an end. We must seek the source of all goodness and love for the fulfillment of our potential — i.e., as one made to the likeness of God.

St. Peter tells us that we have the potential to participate in the divine nature: "For indeed His divine power has granted us all things pertaining to life and piety through the knowledge of Him Who has called us by His own glory and power—through which He has granted us the very great and precious promises, so that through them you may become partakers of the divine nature" (2 Peter: 1:3-4). St. Augustine, a true student of St. Peter, spoke of a human capacity for relationship with God. He spoke of a power and happiness that enables a person to rise not only above human limitations, but even from the depths of a despair induced by personal sin and disorder. The supernatural capacity for happiness and peace springing from the presence of grace (i.e., the divine life) cannot be attained by anything in the created order. Without God we are incomplete, and our longing for happiness remains unsatisfied. In union with God, we begin to take on some characteristics of God the Son. Only through the realization of this love of God expressed in our soul can we begin to understand the command of Christ: "Be you perfect as my heavenly Father is perfect."

Christianity is far more than freeing us from the restrictions of mortal life and immeasurably deeper than the greatest attainments of the natural human potential. Through union with Christ, Christians are essentially oriented toward God. They do not suffer from the illusion of an earthly paradise, nor do they despair from the delusion of an unmerited predestined eternal happiness or unhappiness.

The disparity between the divine knowledge and power and human freedom and potential can be understood only in the mystery of the Incarnation. Karl Adams considers Christ bridging an ontological distance: "Christ binds God and His creation into such a close reciprocal relationship that he cancels and overcomes not only every abyss between God and His creation but also the infinite disparity that separates them by their very natures. Christ conquers...ontological distance"—i.e., the distance between the supreme, all-loving, and perfect Being Who is God, and the limited human who through creative love is called into being with a destiny of knowing God as He is in eternity.

St. Paul in his first letter to the Corinthians tells us how we make this journey through mortal life to eternity as we begin the next chapter.

Chapter XII

❦

The Reality
of Life and
Human Dignity

Please read from the First Letter to the Corinthians 12:31-13:13 as we being our discussion of the source of life and the appreciation of human dignity. The lyric prose in which St. Paul speaks on the centrality of love is more than an ideal it is a call to every person to attain the goal of eternal happiness through love for which God created us. In the pursuit of this goal, we are never alone but move together in a faith community that we call the Church.

Since Vatican II we have been described as a Pilgrim Church, and that is well said—for life is a pilgrimage. We are on the march, and sooner or later we shall reach our destination. That destination we call heaven. There we will see God as He is, and that experience will fulfill our quest for happiness that will be complete and have no end.

In the previous chapter we recognized that no attainment in this life can offer complete and perfect happiness, yet spontaneously we all seek that goal. For this destiny we have eternally existed in the mind of God. The people with whom we relate and influence, members of our family and friends, who possibly have made us role models, hopefully will have realized that this also is their destiny. Integral in our mission in faith is to help them on their journey through life.

While we are on the road, we cannot help wondering about God. What is He like? What does He want from us? What does He expect from us? How can we come to grips with the mystery of God?

We fall sometimes into a simplistic approach. We learn from revelation that we are made to the image and likeness of God. Yet, sometimes He seems to become for us a sort of a benevolent grandfather. This technically is called anthropo-morphism. Unconsciously we think of God in the beauty of His creation and in the unselfish love of family and friends. We know that this is an inadequate analogy. But we still hope—that if only we could see God.

Goodness, truth and beauty that we recognize and appreciate in our friends and neighbors are manifestations of the glory of God the Creator. But goodness, truth, and beauty of character are not physical, they are spiritual. God has given us a spiritual soul that enables us to transcend the physical in order to understand reality and truth and to experience love and beauty.

God also reveals Himself to us in our spontaneous long-ing for perfection, for happiness, for immortality. A small child, when he or she recognizes himself or herself as a unique person, seeks relationships, expresses personal de-sires, and hopes for love. Every person is born with these gifts and desires. They are natural spiritual qualities that makes us human and enable us to relate with each other.

Experiencing love is essential if we are to begin to know God. Many of us feel a bit uneasy, for we have not experi-enced a love for God in a manner as we love a wife, husband, parent, child or friend. Yet when we speak of love, we mean something very noble, very deep and very pure. When I love a person, I do not want to lose either my loving or the one I love. I hope that this love will bring me happiness and go on forever. However, a human loving relationship passes. I can only find permanent happiness and love from God Himself, the source of my very being, Who also is the purpose of my existence.

I am a pilgrim through life, restless at times, but always looking and searching for that which will make me truly and fully myself. While I recognize that I am distinct and differ-ent than everyone else and to that extent have personal autonomy I also recognize that I am dependent and incomplete. I depend on God for my existence. I depend on God to attain the purpose of my life.

In the previous chapters, regardless of their particular theme or focus, an effort was always present to try to probe the "Mystery of God," the " 'Why' of Creation," and our personal situation with both. Because we always seek happiness and peace, we are worried about the causes of personal and societal disorders while we hope for answers. Evidence seems to indicate that we live in an atmosphere of modern idolatry—i.e., confusing pleasure with love, and freedom with license. When this happens, the data suggest that large segments of our society are dominated by money or sensual pleasure, and as a result often become enslaved by that which they seek.

Initially in seeking answers a paradox seems to exist: on the one hand, everything created by God is good; and on the other hand, sin and disorder exist. When a particular gift of God is misused, isolated from the whole, it absorbs the possessor who is in the pursuit of personal satisfaction and thus becomes an end rather than a means and becomes a controlling factor in life.

In apostolic time, St. Paul writing to St. Timothy addressed this fact and stated in his letter: "Every creature of God is good, and nothing to be rejected, but rather to be received with thanksgiving" (Timothy 4:4). The answer lies in the orientation of love of and for God. We read in the Gospel of St. Matthew: "Seek ye first the kingdom of God and His justice and all these things shall be added to you" (Matthew 6:33).

Faithful Christians accept the beauty of creation, the companionship of family and friends, the growth in knowledge and the benefits of the arts and sciences with appreciation and joy. However, they do not take any particular project, recognition, or acclaim too seriously because these activities are not the source or end of reality, but are transient and a means to an end in this journey through life. Our decisions and activities are never isolated because we are social beings. Creation came from the Father through the Son, Who created us as social beings. He also founded the Church in such a manner that we would relate one with the other as a community bonded by faith and love.

Our Lord Jesus Christ came into the world and in His teaching enables each of us to recognize the difference between temporal and eternal values and to regain and maintain our capacity for free choice. However, He does not force His gifts on us.

When we accept His grace, His redemptive love, ultimately we are able to withstand any pressure or spiritual disorder we encounter. The deep question of evil in life is not: Why does God permit sin? Rather, the true questions is: Why did He give us the gift of free will that we so often misuse? An answer to this question, which obviously we do not fully understand, is that He created us to His likeness that we may have a capacity for love and happiness. Love and happiness are not possible without freedom.

Free will is a faculty of the soul and is spiritual in nature. Without this spiritual power, every decision we make would be the result of our physical nature and the conditioning of our experience and environment. Because of our soul we can transcend any physical or material experience. This transcendence is recognized in our ordinary experience. Most decisions and every act can evoke a question or an opinion. Each of our experiences occurs within the limited horizons of personal understanding.

Inasmuch as we constantly move beyond particular experience and can look to the future, we cannot measure our potential for growth, for virtue, for happiness. The more questions and answers we have, the greater possibilities we have for free decisions and personal growth. We have particular goals and objectives in life, but when we attain them we are never fully satisfied. We seek perfect happiness, yet particular persons or accomplishments never fully satisfy our longings. With St. Augustine we can say: "Our hearts are restless, O Lord, and will not rest until they rest in Thee."

The world and every person in the world was called into existence by God as an expression of love. The human response to God's love is never static and it must be shared with others. Of its very nature love is diffusive. Together with faith, love is the bonding force of any community, especially the community of the Church. This faith and love transcends time and personal limitations of each generation and century. God loves each person and, because of His love, each one possesses a unique value; yet in God's providence each attains spiritual growth only in communion with all others who are also so united in and with God.

Christ made this clear in His discourse with the apostles immediately before His passion:

> I do not pray for them alone. I pray also for those who will believe in Me through their word that all may be one, as You, Father, are in Me and I in You; I pray that they may be one in Us that the world may believe that You sent Me.
>
> I have given them the glory. You gave Me that they may be one, as We are one—I living in them, You living in Me, that their unity may be complete.
>
> So shall the world know that You sent Me, and that You loved them as You loved Me. (John 17:20-23)

We men and women of the human family will have attained our destiny when we so unite our freedom to divine providence as to make the will of God our will. That was the prayer of Jesus before He gave us the supreme example of giving His life for us.

How do we evaluate ourselves? Our personality and character will grow and deepen in direct proportion to our acceptance of the grace and will of God. This growth occasions a fundamental insight into reality, into the order of existence, into the relationship between God and each of us. It also involves a judgment and acceptance of our dependence on God; not a dependence of servility, but a dependence of security.

Only through the virtue of humility can a person attain the security of being (i.e., existence) that is essential for true happiness. The humble person judges himself in relation to God, and in the process understands that, separated from God, life has little meaning and purpose. Each person is unique. In sharing in the life of God, each person has a dignity that no one can dismiss. He or she will then recognize that others also have this personal relationship with God. Then one will not compare himself or herself with others to appreciate personal worth. Charity and humility are mutually supportive, and bring about a freedom in action coupled with a freshness and creative insight into the nature of reality—i.e., a world and universe that belongs to God.

A humble person looks to the world not with the pessimism resulting from human failure, but with the potential resulting from divine bounty. Failure is only temporary, and will never completely control a person who knows that he or she can rise with Christ. Possibly because of some circumstance, cultural difference or prejudice a person will not be welcome by different groups. Neither was Christ. Christ warned that such would be the case: "The disciple is not above the master, nor the servant above his lord. It is enough for the disciple to be as his master and the servant as his lord" (Matthew 10:24, 25).

Therefore, humility is not an ideal which remains static, but an attitude and insight that pervades every decision and action of human intercourse. This is possible, even with our tendency to be self-serving, because Our Lord gave the world a new concept of existence beyond the order of time. His existence as man, primarily, was that of Redeemer. He was sent by His heavenly Father to redeem those of us who people this earth and to give to us a vision of eternal existence and eternal participation in being.

This knowledge and participation in the eternal life of God begins in time, but transcends our mortal participation of this measure of existence in time. The gifts and virtues of faith and charity enable us to receive this union with Christ. Knowledge from and through Christ gives us an insight into reality. Frustration and sadness will only be temporary because the recipients of these gifts and insights can rise above self-centeredness. Anyone and all who receive these gifts and practice these virtues will live in the real world that God created. Accurate judgments are made, and the whole pattern of existence has meaning.

The providence of God is both the source and explanation of existence. Through grace, a person is brought into a relationship existing between God the Father and God the Son and God the Holy Spirit. To the degree that a person accepts grace, to that degree does that person participate in the divine existence. The nature and character of human existence is transformed, not changed. Each human being remains a person with a separate identity and responsibility.

At the same time, God draws each person to Himself in a relationship that gives meaning to human personality. In union with God, no one is confined to the knowledge and happiness of the world, for in that union our potential is to partake of the knowledge and freedom of the world's creator. During this life of grace, the new-found freedom acquires a more permanent orientation and formation. Christ called it "a victory which overcomes the world."

Permanent participation in being and therefore the reality of existence is accomplished in this victory. In death, the temporal nature of human existence ceases. Organic life, subject to the physical laws of nature, comes to an end. An understanding of a permanent participation in the existence of God is correlative to an understanding of the soul, as created in the likeness of God. The soul, a spiritual being, has the capacity for truth and goodness.

In the final judgment on the use of freedom, Divine Providence will reveal the dignity and nature of a human being who will permanently participate in the divine life. Whether in life or in eternity, human existence is never separated from the creative and sustaining providence of God. Eternal existence is determined by God when, in His infinite judgment, He calls us into being and grants us immortality. The verdict of salvation completes the work of providence and creation.

This is the ground and root of our movement through life. Rest and peace, happiness and security, are our gifts from God. Our acceptance calls for self-surrender. All love requires surrender, but being in love with God is without limits or qualifications, conditions or reservations. Hopefully, we will attain this in the last moments of our life when, without any hesitation, we surrender our decision-making and destiny to God.

"Eye has not seen nor ear heard, nor has it entered into the heart of man what God has prepared for those who love Him."

Epilogue

As I indicated in the introduction, I had not intended to write a book. As I now reflect on the content as one chapter followed the other, the book is a history of my thought process on the meaning of life and of faith as it was lived in succeeding decades by my family, fellow students from grade school through the university and seminary, in every parish to which I was assigned, and in the four dioceses in which I lived and worked. This epilogue is designed to put in perspective the ideas, the events, and the circumstances that shaped the teachings and understanding of faith that I have presented.

My family, parents, brothers, and sisters provided a security where love was always present and supportive, where the purpose of life was accepted without question and religion was not an abstraction but the God-given means of moving through time to eternity. My parents shared their religious values by example and encouraged me, my three brothers, and my three sisters, to think in terms of the needs of others. Opportunities were always present, for this was the period of the Great Depression following the bank failures of 1929. Mother and dad recognized the possibility of my vocation to the priesthood and encouraged me while at the same time challenged me to accept the realities of a lifelong commitment.

I was blessed in the seminary by a dedicated faculty and one outstanding professor—a priest, Father Joseph Buckley, whose philosophical and theological insight challenged his students to make judgments, think for themselves and work so that the truths of religion and philosophy became integral to one's understanding of life.

My first pastor after ordination in 1940 was a good man, certainly not a scholar, but had the capacity to reach out to people, recognize their abilities, and lead them to become effective and active members of the parish. That was my introduction to collegiality, although he had never heard of the word. He also taught me by his example how to live with mistakes. Because he was impulsive, he made quite a few. However, he did not let them deter him from his work and objectives.

World War II, particularly with the bombing of Pearl Harbor, shocked our country. The mobilization of men and women in the military services and industry called for the involvement of young and old. I was a priest of the time; so many young men of the parish were called to service that it was the most natural action for me to volunteer as an army chaplain. Living in the presence of violence and death for almost three years affects value systems, personality, and character. I was not immune from these influences. In combat, everyone lived in fear. The quality of leadership among the officers from the platoon lieutenant to the three-star general determined in which circumstances people would live or die. Character and competence varied as in civilian life. Incompetence caused mistakes and people died. At the time I did not realize its effect on my life in the future. Strangely, the effect was good—I learned to respect and follow leaders not because of their title or office, but because of their integrity and proper use of their talents. This proved to be a great freeing experience of my life. I had to use the same criteria in evaluating myself. Obviously I have made mistakes, even mistakes that adversely affected the lives of others. I hope that they have been honest mistakes.

The providence of God is always with us when we make decisions that seriously affect our lives. Sometimes we even make the right decisions for the wrong reason. At the end of the war, we all wanted to return home to a normal life. I recognized that almost three years of combat did not exactly prepare me for parish life. I also had been away from serious reading for three years. Returning to graduate school seemed to offer a solution. That decision again changed the pattern and direction of my priestly life. It led me to campus ministry at Louisiana State University in Baton Rouge, Louisiana; seminary work, and teaching philosophy and theology. I spent more than twenty delightful years trying to keep ahead of students, and at least abreast of the ideas of the faculty. In psychology and sociology, logical positivism at that time was a dominant influence. That influence, so negative for spiritual growth of the undergraduates, forced me to continue study so that I could be a help to students as they asked basic questions in this important period of their lives.

Next came a return to parish life in 1962 as pastor of two parishes—Holy Family in Port Allen and St. Joseph Cathedral in Baton Rouge. These parishes were so different in character and membership that I was forced to listen and pray before making decisions which would affect the lives of parishioners either negatively or positively. The first was in a semi-rural parish in the plantation section of south Louisiana. Integration of the races was in its initial stage, but attempts were feeble. I found in the parish church a roped-off section for black parishioners. What could be done about the situation without causing a riot? I hoped that I was capable of listening to the Holy Spirit. Without raising the issue, I bought a can of coal oil, took the ropes down, and burned them. The lay leaders of the parish thought that while theoretically I might be right, I was imprudent. It took six months to a year for people to feel some comfort to intermingle, even while praying.

The second parochial assignment was that of pastor of the Cathedral and at the same time rector of the minor seminary. I discovered in the two jobs I was not as capable as thought I was. I began to learn how to let go and delegate. It was a pleasant experience to learn how capable and dedicated people were. Vatican II's description of the church as the "People

167

of God" became real in that small corner of the Universal Church.

Speaking of Vatican II, that also was a wonderful learning and spiritual experience. I was pleasantly surprised to be invited to Rome in 1961 to work on some of the documentation, especially as applied to priests and bishops. I didn't make much of a contribution, but was exposed to the diversity of cultures and decision processes of priests throughout the world. Some of my smugness, to use a slang expression, was watered down. That was good for the soul.

They say virtue has its rewards. Maybe exposure also has its rewards, as I was invited by my bishop to attend the last session of the Council as a minor-peritus. Again, my primary responsibility was listening. That is not to say that I did not make some private judgments. My first judgment proved to be absolutely wrong. The primary debate and discussion in depth was "The Church in the Modern World." As I listened, I thought in no way can these almost three thousand bishops come to an agreement. Three thousand men in positions of authority with the diversity of language, cultures, and pressures with normal human limitations could not possibly agree on a document that called for such a radical change of understanding the Church in action. I don't remember the exact vote, but it was something like almost three thousand in favor and seventeen against. The Holy Spirit does work within the Church!

I came home to the Cathedral from the Council excited about the potential for the Church. We had already remodeled the sanctuary with the altar facing the congregation, engaged people with professional competence in music and the liturgy, and then I fell on my face. I had moved too fast, but it was a learning experience. One year later when I was called to be the first bishop of a new Diocese of Orlando, Florida. I moved more slowly.

The second project after the Council proved more successful because I had some teaching experience. Who are we as a Church? The two great teaching documents on ecclesiology, "The Constitution on the Church" and "The Church in the Modern World," offered an opportunity to conduct classes for diocesan leaders and graduate students of Louisiana State University. The response was rewarding, especially after the lack of enthusiasm for my first efforts at implementing liturgical changes.

Teaching these two classes on the ecclesiastical documents from Vatican II proved to be an excellent preparation to start the new Diocese of Orlando. I had not been in Orlando more than three months when I thought there should have been some on-the-job training before accepting such a responsibility. To a certain extent, I did have an opportunity to learn how to start a new diocese in my relationship with three bishops and with an associate of mine, who later was to become a bishop. One was a father figure, Archbishop Joseph Rummel; one had a touch of genius in ecclesiology, Bishop Robert Tracy; one was a close friend and companion, Bishop Joseph Vath; and one was a saint, Bishop Stanley Ott.

The father figure ordained me, authorized me to become an army chaplain, sent me to graduate school, and appointed me to some challenging assignments. I worked closely with the second bishop after Vatican II and saw how the Church could become alive by realizing the Church is a people of God on a journey through time to eternity. The third bishop I mentioned above knew my weaknesses and strengths, my successes and failures, and my disappointments and hopes. He was a good listener and always leveled with me. The fourth bishop had been my associate in two different assignments. In the ten years we lived together I never heard him speak unkindly of any person. His prayer life, kindness, dedication, and personal example influenced people in all walks of life—Catholics, Protestants, and Jews. His death was a celebration of his life by the entire community. Living with him for ten years forced me to honestly look at myself.

The necessity to try to be objective and recognize my limitations as well as my gifts was very important in this period of life. I received a letter from the Apostolic Delegate that the Holy Father was establishing a new diocese in Central Florida and intended to appoint me as its first bishop. The letter came as a complete surprise for a number of reasons. My knowledge of Orlando, the See City, was at best vague. I knew it was located somewhere between the Atlantic Ocean and the Gulf of Mexico. I had not moved in circles where bishops were appointed. I was not an auxiliary bishop, had not studied in Rome, and had never worked in a Chancery Office. However, after consulting with my confessor and doing a bit of soul searching, I accepted the challenge and have never regretted it.

The new diocese was rather large in territory and growing in population. This growth created interesting and sometimes confusing family and social situations. The native Floridians—whose livelihood depended on citrus groves, farming, and cattle—were stable and conservative. New families, mostly professionals working in the space programs and industry headquarters for insurance, tended to be progressive but without the support of the extended family. A third group, hard to categorize, worked in service and tourist positions that by the very nature of the demands occasioned large turnover of employment. Many children hardly knew their grandparents.

Pastors, religious educators, and other ministers needed to think creatively to involve these different groups in liturgy, religious education, and social outreach. While starting a new diocese provides an opportunity to look to the future, thank God so much that is good already was in place and active in the faith community. This was very evident in Orlando. Catholic Charities was well-staffed with knowledgeable professionals and volunteers. The National Council of Catholic Women was active with the largest parish membership that I had ever encountered. An excellent Catholic school system was in place, both on an elementary and secondary level.

Population growth called for new parishes. New parishes required pastors that the new diocese did not have. Fortunately, former bishops of the St. Augustine Diocese had contacts with seminaries in Ireland and Spain. A generous response came from these seminaries. The result was that our presbyterate reflected three distinct cultures—American, Irish, and Spanish. Certainly that offered enrichment to the diocese, but it also occasioned difficulties. Different understanding of the Church in action, different comfort levels in collegiality, and diverse methods of religious education made planning and diocesan policy move slowly. Unfortunately, decision-making and diplomacy did not always occur at the same time. However, God's providence was always present; we belonged to the same church and somehow came to a reasonable agreement.

These were the early days of parish councils. We learned as we went along. In one large parish, the members of the first parish council soon discovered that they were split down the middle on most policy decisions. Timing was not the best, and the pastor had a heart attack. The parish council president called a meeting and made the observation that together they could have contributed to the heart attack, and suggested that they vote themselves out of existence. They did agree on that recommendation. A new parish council was elected and it worked.

Another difficulty was my lack of knowledge regarding

Canon Law. That at first did not bother me too much until I discovered that we did not have a professional canonist in the new diocese. My conscience raised its head and suggested that I had better check up on myself. I happily made decisions based on my understanding of the church and theology. Then periodically, about 10 p.m. each night, I called my friend Bishop Joe Vath who had a background in law, told him of my decisions and asked if I was still legitimate. The next year I sent a priest to Catholic University in Washington to study Canon Law.

The new diocese was immediately faced with the serious needs of several thousand migrant workers. Entire families worked in the citrus groves. Religious education, health care, housing, and advocacy with the state of Florida presented problems that no single religious, business, or political entity could possibly answer. We did not come up with all the answers, but made some progress. Four sisters of the Congregation of Notre Dame de Namur, two sisters from Cuba, and two priests from Spain worked in different areas of health clinics, religious education programs, subsidized housing, and Sunday liturgies. Even among the migrants there was class distinction and different family values among Mexican Americans, African Americans, and white imports from Appalachia. Each group had to be recognized as coming from a background peculiar to themselves and afforded the dignity that everyone deserves.

Since Orlando as a diocese was in its infancy, people seemed to expect some changes, so the time was appropriate to implement the Vatican Council document, "The Church in the Modern World." Priests Council, Sisters Council, Diocesan Education Committee, Associated Catholic Charities Committees were in place after about a year. The dedication and competence of parishioners in all walks of life was a pleasure to experience. Of course, not all were immediately successful. But I believe that growing pains basically are healthy.

Six pleasant years rolled by, and I was surprised to learn that the Holy Father, Pope Paul VI, suggested I move to Baltimore, the mother diocese of the church in the United States. The kindness and confidence of the Holy Father certainly was appreciated, but again called for personal evaluation. About that time I was returning from California from a religious education convention and stopped by the newsstand to find a mystery paperback, which is my customary reading for long flights, to ease the journey back to Florida. Instead, I selected a book titled *The Peter Principle*. Allow me to refresh your memory: The theme of the book offers the thesis that some people rise up the ladder of business or profession to their level of incompetence. That is, some people are promoted and then they have taken one step beyond their ability and meet disaster. While possibly the book was written with tongue in cheek, an element of truth was present. I made a couple of meditations about moving from a small diocese to the venerable Church of Baltimore.

Nature seemed to be crying as I made three trips to Baltimore in 1974 to discuss the condition and direction of the archdiocese with Lawrence Cardinal Shehan and diocesan officials for it rained heavily during all three occasions. The rich history of the Church of Baltimore and the resources found in two major seminaries, three Catholic colleges, twenty-three Catholic high schools, seventy-two elementary schools, religious education programs, Catholic hospitals, nursing homes, comprehensive programs of Catholic Charities, and a good archdiocesan newspaper suggested that the new archbishop could relax and admire the marvelous work of so many dedicated people.

Such was not the case. Within two months the Baltimore sanitation workers and police went on strike. Their efforts to seek better working conditions and increased pay had merit, but chaos almost resulted. I soon learned that the archbishop was expected to get involved in civic affairs.

The next difficulty created even more tension when a court ruling to effect integration required children to be bused to various public schools. After discussing the possible dangers with archdiocesan and city leaders, it was suggested that I make an appeal through the medium of television for calm in working toward policies that were the best for the children. The three television stations offered time and the response from parents was excellent. One suggestion that proved effective was that a representative number of parents ride the buses for a few weeks. Volunteers accepted the suggestion and relative calm was reached.

These experiences again brought home the reality that the Gospel must be proclaimed in such a manner that people would recognize that Christ was present to them regardless of their experiences, good or bad, whether others approved of them or rejected them. God's love is not conditioned by human limitations.

My personal limitations became very evident at this time. Only six months after coming to Baltimore, while making a retreat at a Trappist Monastery in Berryville, Virginia, I suffered a serious heart attack. Mortality came home to me very strongly. My priorities in life and my vocation again came into sharp focus.

Convalescence occasioned a time for reflection on the mission of the Church of Baltimore of which I was to be an active member for the next fifteen-plus years. In pastoral letters, I reflected on both personal and communal responsibilities. Some of the topics and issues I addressed received wide attention. For example, I wrote a pastoral letter on prayer in which I expressed my belief that prayer is absolutely essential for spiritual growth that rests on a love relationship with

God. In another letter, I discussed the understanding of conscience, which parallels the implementation of personal responsibility, peace of mind, justice, and charity. In my pastoral on collegiality, I noted that the church is the largest volunteer organization in the world so a recognition of the vocation of the laity, of all the baptized and confirmed, and their gifts in living and proclaiming the Gospel is essential for our church to be alive and well. In another pastoral I noted that throughout history in most countries, including our own, the gifts of women have not been properly recognized and opportunities have not been provided. These pastoral realities and many others were the subject of pastoral letters written as occasion seemed to warrant.

I asked, through pastoral letters, that the faith community of the Archdiocese accept a "spiritual given" that every Christian is involved in mission, and the Church in its totality has a missionary task. A person cannot accept the gift of God's love without sharing that love with one's neighbor. Inherent in that love is Christ's commission "to teach all nations" without the limits of any culture or boundaries. No member of the Church is alive for himself or herself alone. Each has a function of service to offer and give to others — not only for members of the faith community, but for everyone.

In faith I believed, in study I learned, and in pastoral responsibility I taught the eternal truth that Christ came into the world to offer redemption to all men and women. Each of us of the faith community has an obligation to reach out and share our faith with others. Our state of life, work, and social relationships will provide opportunities that, please God, we will be able to recognize. We need to observe and listen.

My motto when appointed bishop was *Auscultabo ut Serviam*—i.e., I will listen that I may serve. Living up to this motto proved necessary in long-range planning, decisions in crisis, and finding the right leaders on both archdiocesan and parish levels. Thank God people were available and they were dedicated and loyal to the mission of the archdiocese. Mistakes were made, and trying to correct them (since at times this negatively affected peoples' lives) was very painful. For example, an easy way does not exist in asking someone to resign. Good intentions and capabilities at times do not match; personality conflicts have not been resolved; financial restraints require cutbacks in personnel — these conditions and other human limitations at times are beyond control. Yet, for the good of all decisions must be made. Perfect balance and perfect justice exists only in the next world. I have learned the hard way that just as pain tells us that something is wrong with the body, suffering tells us that something is out of balance in the soul.

Growth requires change, and change demands that priorities must be developed. Priorities emerged during my tenure as archbishop: religious education; support of family life; outreach to teenagers; programs for the poor; response to financial needs for Catholic schools; advocacy for vocations to the priesthood and religious life; the role of leadership for women in the church; coupled with a collegial approach to answering each of these needs. In responding to these priorities as we continued to accept the mission that Christ gave us, we looked to the future with confidence. That confidence rests on the promise of Christ to remain with us until the end of time. He did not tell us that it would always be easy, but He did say: "I will be with you always."

Together we priests, religious, and lay leaders learned that we and all of the People of God are a faith community of volunteers helping each other move through the order of time to the omega point of existence, a perfect union with God in eternity. For we have learned from Sacred Scripture: "Eye has not seen nor ear heard nor has it entered into the heart of man what God has prepared for those who love Him."

About the Author

Archbishop William D. Borders was born in 1913 in the farming community of Washington, Indiana. He started studying for the priesthood in 1932, and was ordained in 1940 at St. Louis Cathedral, New Orleans, Louisiana. Three years later, he enlisted in the U.S. Army Chaplain Corps and served in Africa and Italy before leaving the service with the rank of major.

In 1947, he received a master of science degree in education from the University of Notre Dame. He continued working in the higher education community as a chaplain on the campus of Louisiana State University until 1964 when he was named rector of St. Joseph Cathedral, Baton Rouge. During this time, he was also a participant in Vatican II.

On May 2, 1968, Pope Paul VI named him founding Bishop of Orlando, Florida. Six years later, he transfered to Baltimore where he was named Archbishop of the "Premier See," Mother Church of American Catholicism.

Archbishop Borders served the Church and the Archdiocese of Baltimore for fifteen years, until his retirement in 1989. He continues to teach and lecture.